Mallard returned to steam between March 25, 1986, and August 27, 1988, and hauled a special train on July 3, 1988 to mark the exact 50th anniversary of its world record run. One of the main reasons why the National Railway Museum decided not to resteam it for the 75th anniversary was the fact that there are three A4s operating on the main line today, and adding a fourth would not make commercial sense. In 1986, it hauled a series of British Rail dining train trips from Marylebone to Stratford-upon-Avon and back, and on October 26 that year was seen passing Blackthorn, Oxfordshire, on one of them. JOHN TITLOW

Contents

CHAPTER 1
6   Introduction

CHAPTER 2
14   Mallard 75 by royal appointment

CHAPTER 3
20   The ones that got away

CHAPTER 4
40   *Mallard* on tour

CHAPTER 5
48   Doncaster Museum remembers the speed kings

CHAPTER 6
52   The Autumn Great Gathering

CHAPTER 7
60   They made it happen!

CHAPTER 8
64   New light on the steam era's finest

CHAPTER 9
70   Sons of *Mallard*

CHAPTER 10
78   *Bittern* timed at 94

CHAPTER 11
84   The rebirth of 'The Cross'

CHAPTER 12
90   Giants of the Roundhouse

CHAPTER 13
102   The electric 'Mallard'

CHAPTER 14
104   The Great Goodbye

CHAPTER 15
122   The magnificent seven

CHAPTER 16
124   A new Gresley masterpiece for the 21st century

MALLARD
THE MAGNIFICENT SIX

Author:
Robin Jones

Designers:
Tim Pipes, Libby Fincham, Charlotte Pearson

Reprographics:
Jonathan Schofield, Simon Duncan

Group production editor:
Tim Hartley

Production manager:
Craig Lamb

Marketing manager:
Charlotte Park

Publishing director:
Dan Savage

Commercial director:
Nigel Hole

Published by:
**Mortons Media Group Ltd,
Media Centre,
Morton Way, Horncastle,
Lincolnshire LN9 6JR**
Tel: 01507 529529

Printed by:
**William Gibbons and Sons,
Wolverhampton**

Credits:

All pictures marked * are published under a Creative Commons licence. Full details may be obtained at http://creativecommons.org/licences

ISBN 978-1-909128-43-9

All material copyright Mortons Media Limited, 2014. All rights reserved.

MORTONS MEDIA GROUP LTD

Foreword

Being invited to write a contribution to a railway magazine, periodical or journal is something that happens from time to time, so Robin Jones's request that I put pen to paper and draft the foreword to this commemorative publication did not at first perplex me.

After all, I had been mildly involved with the Mallard 75 project and therefore knew the 'story' inside out, so recounting the chronology of events would be straightforward. But on closer examination I began to get a real sense that the task set me was actually quite difficult.

The challenge from my perspective was how to convey, in terms which could not be judged exaggerated or over-superlative, the supreme importance, both domestically and internationally, of what we have all just witnessed.

How do I maintain an element of objectivity and rational calm in describing a truly remarkable venture (see, I've already breached the principle!). But try as I might, it really is very difficult not to be triumphalist and hugely celebratory about what has occurred.

For Mallard 75 just might come to be viewed in the years ahead as the event that changed forever the nature of how the great British public perceives railway heritage and railway enthusiasm.

Mallard's record-breaking anniversary had to be celebrated, that's for sure. But the 75th birthday called for something seriously imaginative, particularly as there was no prospect of the locomotive being returned to traffic for the event.

At a time of national austerity, perhaps the country needed a lift; to be reminded of its considerable engineering achievements. Perhaps our contemporary railway network needed a celebratory shot in the arm around which it could fully unite with the railway heritage movement? Or then again was it a time for the National Railway Museum to demonstrate its world-leading status, and employ its corporate and reputational muscle to make something very special happen?

I suppose all of these motives were present to varying degrees. Whatever the principal motive, this has nevertheless been a project which fundamentally flew on the back of an innate gut instinct that the sheer audacity of assembling all six surviving A4s would capture the public imagination.

There was no market-tested analysis involved; no business case looking at the commercial viability of such an operation; and certainly no fallback plan in the event that sponsorship was not forthcoming.

No, this was a project that depended for success on a vision, compellingly articulated, that potential sponsors and supporters alike would feel instinctively drawn to. A vision that made clear that this was all about the best of British. A vision that the overseas organisations involved would feel they did not wish to miss out on. And a vision which was clear in its aim that this seminal anniversary should become a vehicle to reach out to the overwhelmingly non-enthusiast majority of this country.

The fact that two of the locomotives involved were on the other side of the Atlantic simply added to the project's attraction, with the sense of escalating dramatic expectation as their complex journey was undertaken being an essential ingredient. Let's be clear, it was the transatlantic dimension that made Mallard 75 the success it has become.

If all six locomotives had been UK-based, then the 'impossible' nature of Mallard 75 would have been seriously diluted – future reunions would always have been a possibility. This never-to-be-repeated aspect of the project was one of the key messages.

Although much of the subsequent focus has been on *Dwight D. Eisenhower* and *Dominion of Canada*, paradoxically the most important first step in organising Mallard 75 was not to approach our opposite numbers in Green Bay and Montreal, but to write confidentially to the private owners of *Sir Nigel Gresley*, *Union of South Africa* and *Bittern* outlining the plan, swearing them to secrecy, and asking for their agreement to take part.

If only one of them had declined then the whole point of the exercise would have been defeated and it would have been pointless even discussing the matter with our North American allies. I am delighted to report that they all replied in the affirmative by return of post.

Mallard's participation as a national asset was a given, but I think we should be collectively grateful that the private owners of the UK-based locomotives so readily took part in the proceedings with what must have been an impact on their respective income streams. They shared the vision and helped make it a reality.

Ambitious plans need a sprinkling of heroes to make them happen. This story is no different. It was heroic of the National Railroad Museum, Green Bay, and Exporail, the Canadian Railway Museum in Montreal to entrust their precious locomotives to the care of the National Railway Museum in the first place.

The Friends of the National Railway Museum were equally heroic in trusting their instincts and investing in the cosmetic restoration of our transatlantic visitors, thus helping to secure one of the conditions of loan.

The actual restoration of the locomotives was heroic, and much praise should be heaped in particular on the now-famous 'blue team' at Shildon whose work to convert *Dominion of Canada* to fully valanced 1937 condition complete with single chimney, chrome fittings, CPR Bell and chime whistle must rate as one of the more eye-catching aspects of the overall project.

Our many sponsors and supporters pulled together magnificently, but special mention must go to Atlantic Container Line. They really

The A4s A-Team: Steve Davies (left) and haulier Andrew Goodman on board the cargo ship *Atlantic Conveyor* before the unloading of *Dominion of Canada* on October 3, 2012. ROBIN JONES

were central to all this, and their calm and reassuring attitude when we missed the first planned sailing out of Halifax was just what was needed at a very stressful moment.

Assembling the six locomotives was a challenge in itself, but it all had to be brought together in an eye-catching and polished way, and I believe that the National Railway Museum staff at both York and Shildon rose to the challenge in a magnificent way, demonstrating an amazing sense of occasion and delivering what has arguably been the most important railway anniversary event in the preservation era.

Mallard 75 went way beyond the physical confines of York and Shildon, and we should

also recognise the inspired combined efforts of Network Rail, East Coast, other main line operators and *Bittern*'s owners not only to facilitate a remarkable series of high-speed runs but also to enable the movement on Network Rail tracks of a significant number of steam locomotives in a Mallard 75 context. This was truly a whole-railway collaborative achievement. So a lot of heroic action was in evidence from a wide variety of sources.

But the biggest heroes by far were Andrew Goodman and his lads from Moveright International. It is no exaggeration to say that without him and his team none of this would have happened. They were out of the country for over two months, dealing tenaciously with every problem and issue that such a complex move could throw at them, keeping their cool, summoning every ounce of initiative, and doing their utmost to ensure that an excited and expectant British population was not disappointed. Andrew, I and many others owe you a deep debt of gratitude.

So will we ever see anything like this again? I seriously doubt that all six A4s will be assembled in one place ever again. *Dwight D. Eisenhower* and *Dominion of Canada* will soon return to their native shores and to a spectacular welcome home.

They have acted as important ambassadors for their respective owning museums and will be taking pride of place in refreshed gallery spaces where their story can be told to great effect. There will simply be no incentive for them to pay a return visit to the UK for a very long time, if ever. So let us be eternally grateful that Mallard 75 happened in our lifetimes, and we should now use its powerful legacy to maintain the interest and enthusiasm of the many converts it achieved to the railway heritage cause.

Finally, I will be 79 years old for the *Mallard* centenary celebrations in 2038. I said the A4s won't gather again. But if we start planning now...

Steve Davies MBE
Former director, National Railway Museum, York

CHAPTER ONE

Introduction

L.N.E.R.: ENGINE "MALLARD"
THIS ENGINE IS NOTABLE FOR HAVING BEEN USED IN THE SPEED TEST
WHEN 125 MILES PER HOUR WAS REACHED.

LENGTH OVER BUFFERS	71 FT. 3¼ INS.	CYLINDERS (3) DIAMETER	18½ INS.
TOTAL WEIGHT	163 TONS 6 CWTS	STROKE	26 INS.
BOILER PRESSURE	250 LBS/SQ. IN.	TRACTIVE EFFORT	35,455 LBS.
DIAMETER OF DRIVING WHEELS	6 FT. 8 INS.	COAL	9 TONS
	WATER	5,000 GALLONS	

Back in 1972, the British Museum's Treasures of Tutankhamun exhibition set an exacting new standard for events of its type. It ran for six months, and attracted more than 1.6 million visitors, some of them queuing for up to eight hours. The most popular exhibition in the museum's history, it afterwards went on a world tour lasting several years.

The equivalent in the railway heritage sector is the National Railway Museum's Mallard 75. The repatriation of exiled London & North Eastern Railway A4 streamlined Pacific locomotives No. 60008 *Dwight D. Eisenhower* and No. 60010 *Dominion of Canada* (since restored as No. 4489) from across the Atlantic, to join their four surviving sisters to mark the 75th anniversary of No. 4468 *Mallard* setting the

The Great Goodbye: all six surviving LNER A4 streamlined Pacifics lined up at Locomotion: The National Railway Museum at Shildon, on the evening of February 19, one of a series of night-time photographic events held during the event. Left to right are postwar record holder No. 60007 *Sir Nigel Gresley*, No. 60008 *Dwight D. Eisenhower*, No. 60009 *Union of South Africa*, No. 4489 *Dominion of Canada*; heritage era record-holder No. 4464 *Bittern* and world steam speed record holder No. 4468 *Mallard*. FRED KERR

still unbroken world steam railway speed record of 126mph on Stoke Bank in Lincolnshire, likewise caught the public imagination big time.

Following the cosmetic restoration of the temporarily repatriated pair, three line-ups were staged, the first two at the National Railway Museum in York – the Great Gathering and the Autumn Great Gathering – which over a period of around three weeks attracted nearly a quarter of a million visitors. The third line-up, the Great Goodbye, staged at the NRM's outreach station of the Locomotion museum in Shildon, which was originally designed to cater for 60,000 visitors annually, topped that number in the first half of the February 15-23, 2014, event alone.

The Mallard 75 project from inception to conclusion has been one of the truly great railway adventures of the modern age.

As editor of *Heritage Railway* magazine, we heard rumours abroad in early 2011, but it seemed too fantastic for words. We finally broke the story in August that year, and even after it hit the front page, there were many sceptics who maintained it would never happen.

There were those who were not silenced until the transatlantic pair finally returned to home soil at dawn on October 3, 2012, unloaded from the Atlantic Container Line cargo ship *Atlantic Conveyor* at Liverpool's Seaforth Docks, before being taken onward by low-loader to Locomotion.

The Mallard 75 logo displayed on the side of the National Railway Museum in York before the Great Goodbye. NRM

Seventy five years after its world record feat, *Mallard* is still winning awards.

On Friday, April 5, 2013, the locomotive was presented with a coveted Heritage Engineering Award by the Institution of Mechanical Engineers on the anniversary of designer Sir Nigel Gresley's death, in the presence of his grandson Tim Godfrey (left), who was born in the same year as No. 4468 was built.

Helen Ashby, head of knowledge and collections, receives the award from chairman of the Institution's engineering heritage committee, John Wood, on behalf of the National Railway Museum.

John Wood said: "*Mallard* is one of the most iconic engineering artefacts of the 20th century, and an example of British ingenuity at its very best.

"Sir Nigel Gresley showed extraordinary ambition and vision in designing this locomotive and it is testament to the work of the National Railway Museum that this awe-inspiring locomotive remains in such excellent condition.

"*Mallard* is a worthy addition to the recipients of Engineering Heritage Awards which also include the E-Type Jaguar, Tower Bridge and the Avro Vulcan bomber."

Chris Nettleton of the Gresley Society said: "It is testament to Sir Herbert Nigel Gresley's brilliance that one of his locomotive designs captured the world speed crown, marking a pinnacle for British engineering which became a significant marker in global history.

"Gresley is one of the greatest engineers the world has ever known and it is only fitting that his work be recognised." NRM

The National Railway Museum's cutaway replica of Stephenson's *Rocket*, hailed as the world's first 'modern' steam locomotive, overlooks the world's fastest steam at the Autumn Great Gathering at the York venue on November 13, 2013. Around the turntable in the Great Hall are A4s No. 60007 *Sir Nigel Gresley*, No. 60008 *Dwight D. Eisenhower*, No. 60009 *Union of South Africa*, No. 4464 *Bittern*, No. 4468 *Mallard* and No. 4489 *Dominion of Canada*. FRED KERR

THE STORY SO FAR

This book is both the companion volume to, and second part of, *Mallard 75*, which was published in summer 2013. *Mallard 75* the book began with the emergence of the world's first true Pacific (4-6-2) locomotives at the start of the 20th century and ended by covering the first Great Gathering at York, in July 2013.

The first volume looked at the great rivalries between the East and West Coast main lines which erupted in the Races to the North of late Victorian times, followed by a 30-year lull during which there was widespread public concern over train speed, to the explosion of steam locomotive technology in the Thirties.

Nigel Gresley took over from Henry Alfred Ivatt as the Great Northern Railway's locomotive superintendent in 1911. The following year, he produced his first GNR design, the H2 (LNER K1) 2-6-0.

While HA Ivatt's Atlantics had been hugely successful in their day, express passenger trains were becoming too long for them, and after looking in depth at the Pennsylvania Railroad's K4 Pacifics, which first appeared in 1914,

Gresley designed a pair of 4-6-2s for the GNR.

The first of them, No. 1470 *Great Northern*, appeared in 1922, and was followed by No. 1471 *Sir Frederick Banbury*. The design, based on Gresley's universal three-cylinder layout and conjugated valve gear, exploited the East Coast Main Line's loading gauge to the full, with large boilers and wide fireboxes.

Following the Grouping of January 1, 1923, Gresley was appointed as chief mechanical engineer of the GNR's successor, the LNER.

A total of 31 of his A1 Pacifics were built at Doncaster, with a further 30 by North British. No. 1472, later 4472, was named *Flying Scotsman*. The class was followed by the A3 Pacifics, into which all of the original A1s including *Flying Scotsman* were rebuilt.

On May 1, 1928, No. 4472 hauled the 'Flying Scotsman' train all 393 miles from King's Cross to Edinburgh non-stop for the first time. On November 30, 1934, *Flying Scotsman* again entered the record books by becoming the world's first steam locomotive to be officially recorded at 100mph, on Stoke Bank in Lincolnshire.

The LNER and Gresley, however, wanted

more. In 1933, serious competition to the dominance of steam haulage came in the form of the German high-speed diesel-electric two-car railcar set the 'Flying Hamburger', which reached the remarkable speed of 77.4mph.

Gresley was convinced steam could still be just as effective, if not more so, and the LNER chief general manager Sir Ralph Wedgwood suggested that faster speeds could be obtained with an ordinary Pacific engine.

Streamlining was being seen as a way forward, and Gresley was heavily inspired by the shape of Italian racing car designer Ettore Bugatti's petrol railcars designed for French railways. In turn, their aerodynamic shape was based somewhat on his racing cars.

Gresley was given the go-ahead to build a new streamlined train, the 'Silver Jubilee' marking the Silver Jubilee of George V in 1935. The train marked the emergence of a new locomotive, the shape of which was startling and so radically different to anything that had gone before.

No. 2509 *Silver Link* was the first of the A4 Pacifics, which took the A3 concept to the next stage and beyond. On a trial run over the

ECML on September 27, 1935, *Silver Link* twice reached 111-112mph.

Meanwhile, Gresley's counterpart on the LMS, William Stanier, had come up with two classes of world-beating Pacifics, firstly the Princess Royals and then, in the wake of the A4s, the streamlined Princess Coronations. They enabled the LMS 'Royal Scot' express train to compete with the LNER's 'Flying Scotsman'. On June 29, 1937, No. 6220 *Coronation* took the world steam speed record with a top speed of 114mph south of Crewe, and the LMS also claimed the fastest start-to-stop runs of over 100 and 150 miles. The next day, A4 No. 4489 *Dominion of Canada* hauled the LNER's 'Coronation' on its trial run, hitting 109.5mph down Stoke Bank.

Meanwhile, on May 11, 1936, Deutsche Reichsbahn-Gesellschaft's Class 03 Pacific No. 05002 reached 124mph between Berlin and Hamburg, while hauling a VIP special train containing Nazi top brass including Heinrich Himmler and the equally primitive-brained Reinhard Heydrich, architects of the Holocaust. Fearing Hitler would favour road transport, the country's railways wanted to

BRITISH RAILWAYS SOLD *MALLARD'S* SMOKEBOX PLATE FOR 87P!

It is a world transport icon. Yet more than half a century ago, British Railways sold the smokebox numberplate from No. 60022 *Mallard* for just 17/6 – 87½p in today's money.

The price also included free carriage to the buyer's nearest station.

Railwayana collector, Paul Tilley, found the sale recorded in a 3in thick leatherbound Eastern Region ledger of assets sold between January 1962 and May 1964.

Compiled at Doncaster, it appeared that items, which today would be worth tens of thousands of pounds, were sold off at prices seemingly determined by the whim of the clerk rather than historical relevance.

The smokebox numberplate from *Mallard* went for the same price as that from WD 2-8-0 No. 90087 – and for 2s-6d (12½p) less than the smokebox plate from the infinitely humbler LMS 2-6-4T No. 42511.

Other examples listed in the ledger include the sale of a nameplate from A4 No. 60003 *Andrew K. McCosh* for £15-6s in 1963, that from No. 60030 *Golden Fleece* including one of its worksplates for £11-17s-6d and the one from No. 60033 *Seagull* for £9-15s.

In 1964, nameplates from No. 60021 *Wild Swan* and No. 60029 *Woodcock* were sold for £10 each.

During the 29 months covered by the ledger, Doncaster sold 139 nameplates, including nine from A1s, 16 from A2s at mostly £10, 30 from A3s, and 11 from A4s, including No. 60014 *Silver Link* and No. 60015 *Quicksilver*.

prove that they still had a part to play in the Third Reich.

The LNER and Gresley wanted the speed record back, and permanently. On June 28, 1938, Gresley, then 62, requested No. 4468 *Mallard* for use on a test run five days later, but did not specify the real purpose.

Doncaster driver Joe Duddington, 61, and fireman Thomas Bray were told to prepare themselves for a special mission that took place on Sunday, July 3, 1938. A pristine *Mallard*, then only a few months old was coupled to the LNER dynamometer car, and with inspector Sam Jenkins on board, set out northwards from London's Wood Green sidings, at first carrying out braking tests between 90-100mph.

It was only when the test train stopped at Barkston Junction north of Grantham that the real purpose of the trip was made clear to those on board. An attempt at the world speed record.

Duddington knew exactly what had to be done. Accelerating down Stoke Bank, *Mallard* reached 120mph, breaking the LMS record, and for a quarter of a mile, at milepost 90¼ between Little Bytham and Essendine, the needle in the dynamometer car recorded 126mph.

It was said that the windows in Little Bytham station were smashed as the train roared through, spraying the platforms with hot ashes.

Mallard's middle end bearing ran hot and the white metal melted, meaning that it had to be taken off the train at Peterborough. However, when a substitute Ivatt Atlantic reached King's Cross with the train, the national press was waiting and the footplate crew received a heroes' welcome, being immortalised in legend at a stroke. Sadly, Gresley was not on board as he was at home ill.

The press called *Mallard* the 'blue streak', and the term stuck to all 35 members of the class.

Coming out of the recession of the Thirties, Duddington, Bray and Jenkins had delivered exactly what the nation so desperately needed in terms of restoring confidence and boosting morale.

Gresley wanted to have another crack at the record, but was stopped by the outbreak of the Second World War, and died after a short illness on April 5, 1941.

Mallard's record would never be broken, but sister No. 60007 *Sir Nigel Gresley* set an official postwar steam record of 112mph on Stoke Bank on May 23, 1959, hauling a Stephenson Locomotive Society special. Indeed, the 12.3 miles from Corby Glen to Tallington were covered at an average of 104mph, possibly the fastest-ever steam speed timing between those points on Stoke Bank, beating even *Mallard*.

Mallard, as British railways No. 60022, hauled the last nonstop 'The Elizabethan' from King's Cross to Edinburgh on September 8, 1961. It was withdrawn from King's Cross on April 25, 1963, having covered 1,426,261 miles.

With the demise of steam well under way, the British Transport Collection drew up a list of locomotives to be preserved as part of a national collection. The practice was to save the first of the class, in this case *Silver Link*, but *Mallard*'s speed record gave it priority, and so it was saved for future generations.

Magnificent as the A4s were, they did not last three decades in service. The class, like the other ECML Pacifics, succumbed to dieselisation and the power of the English electric Deltics.

Thankfully, three other A4s were preserved in Britain, *Sir Nigel Gresley*, No. 60009 *Union of South Africa*, and No. 60019 *Bittern*.

When No. 60008 *Dwight D. Eisenhower* was withdrawn in 1964, British Railways, which had earlier turned down an offer from Harold E Fuller, the chairman of the National Railroad Museum in Green Bay, Wisconsin, to buy it, happily donated it along with a pair of LNER coaches used by General Eisenhower. It was shipped to the USA on April 27 that year.

For one glorious moment, the Lincolnshire village of Little Bytham on an otherwise sleepy Sunday, July 3, 1938, found itself at the centre of world transport technology, when *Mallard* hit 126mph down Stoke Bank on its fabled speed record run. Here, sister No. *4464 Bittern* heads northbound through the village on December 19, 2013 with the Steam Dreams' 'Cathedrals Express' to York. BRIAN SHARPE

Emerging from Stoke Tunnel, near the scene of *Mallard's* world record run, No. 60009 *Union of South Africa* hauls the Railway Touring Company's 'York Yuletide Express' from Norwich to York and back past High Dyke. BRIAN SHARPE

The world's first railway pub drew on the world's fastest locomotive for the basis of its new sign.

Steven Findlater, landlord of the Railway Tavern, in High Northgate, Darlington, commissioned renowned local artist Ted Parker to create the 4ft sign, which features a vintage-look painting of *Mallard* on one side, and was unveiled in the spring of 2013.

On the reverse is an image of new-build A1 Peppercorn Pacific No. 60163 *Tornado*, the last steam engine to be built in Darlington.

Steven said: "We approached Ted Parker especially because we knew he was a great train artist and the sign is absolutely brilliant.

"This pub is named as the first railway tavern to have been built in the world and it is the only one never to have closed."

No. 60010's name likewise saved it from the scrap man. Withdrawn on May 29, 1965, British Railways donated it to the Canadian Railroad Historical Association. It was shipped to Canada in April 1967, and preserved at Exporail, the Canadian Railway Museum at Delson/Saint-Constant. Near Montreal.

As Britain's railway heritage movement blossomed over the years, several serious offers were made to buy back one or both of the A4s from North America, but all were turned down.

It therefore went without saying that the offer by Steve Davies to borrow them back for a short period and cosmetically restore them was a major breakthrough of phenomenal proportions.

Mallard 75 the book described in detail the meticulous operation to repatriate the pair in 2012, with *Dwight D. Eisenhower* – which had been all but bricked into the Green Bay museum building – having to be slid out sideways by Andrew Goodman's Moveright International team.

After many nerve-racking moments over two months during the summer of 2012, the pair were reunited and on their

In a parallel universe, Britain's railways might have kept steam traction, or at least its most effective forms, into more recent times. Here is Owen Hodgson's 'what might have been' view of two A4 Pacifics in Virgin Trains livery. AC LOCO GROUP/FICTITIOUSLIVERIES.CO.UK

way back home. Taken first to Locomotion for immediate public display, it was clear that the passage of years had taken their toll, at least on their outward appearance. In the Locomotion workshops, *Dominion of Canada* was transformed from its latter-day condition as No. 60010 in faded BR green livery into its original as-built form as No. 4489 in LNER garter blue, complete with valances.

Dwight D. Eisenhower was subsequently moved to the NRM's workshops at York where it was cosmetically restored, keeping its BR appearance, livery and number.

Meanwhile, out on the main line, No. 4464 *Bittern* was given special dispensation to run three trips at 90mph to mark Mallard 75, after successfully undergoing a test run on May 29, 2013. It reached 91.5mph on the runs between Southall and Didcot, and back, on the 15-mile stretch between Didcot East Junction and Tilehouse East Junction, and in doing so set a new official preservation-era steam speed record.

The first of *Bittern*'s three passenger-carrying trips, 'The Ebor Streak' from King's Cross to York, took place on June 29, 2013, and *Bittern* broke its own record with a top speed of 92.5mph at Balderton crossing south of Newark-on-Trent.

After the northbound trip, *Bittern* moved into the NRM yard, ready for the start of the Great Gathering on July 3, 75 years to the day after *Mallard* set the world speed record. And the crowds poured in.

In this second part of the Mallard 75 epic, the story of a truly momentous year continues…

Mallard 75
by royal appointment!

July 22, 2013, was a day that the Prince of Wales for one will never, never forget. Firstly, the patron of the Mallard 75 celebrations arrived in style for a private viewing of the world's fastest steam locomotive and its two repatriated sisters, *Dwight D. Eisenhower* and *Dominion of Canada*, at the National Railway Museum in York.

His visit took place five days after the first Great Gathering had half dispersed, with the three operational A4s leaving to resume their duties.

Prince Charles is renowned as an enthusiast and has been a great friend to the preservation sector. He was given the honour of naming new-build £3 million A1 Peppercorn Pacific No. 60163 *Tornado* at York station on February 19, 2009, after it began its main line career. On that occasion, LNER apple green-liveried *Tornado* hauled the Royal Train, with the prince on the footplate.

However, this time round, it would be an earlier type of East Coast Main Line Pacific, no less than a Gresley A4, which would bring the Royal Train carrying the prince straight into the former York North shed.

And the day would be different to any that had gone before. Because less than 6hr 30min after No. 4464 *Bittern*, proudly carrying the Prince of Wales' coat of arms, headed the train into what is now the NRM's Great Hall at 10am for another reunion with three of its sisters, the prince became a grandfather for the first time.

The visit had been arranged well in advance, and true to his word, the prince kept his engagement.

However, at that time, Catherine, Duchess of Cambridge, had already gone into labour and had been admitted to St Mary's Hospital in London earlier that morning.

During his visit, aides kept the prince supplied with regular updates of her progress.

Bittern and its Mk1 support coach had been attached to the Royal Train in the Siemens rail yard at York, and so made only a short journey on this very special of occasions.

After *Bittern* moved on to the turntable and brought the train to a standstill, the prince alighted and was greeted by Lord Crathorne, the Lord Lieutenant of North Yorkshire, and other civic dignitaries.

He was then introduced to former *Mallard* driver Bernard Bell, 89, who was once fireman on another locomotive hauling the Royal Train with The Queen on board.

"He was very interested in the locomotives and he asked me all sorts of questions about my driving," said Bernard, a former mayor of York. "He seemed very nice."

Left: *Bittern*, still steaming, stands on the turntable in the Great Hall carrying the Prince of Wales' coat of arms. ROBIN JONES

Below: Prince Charles sounds *Mallard*'s whistle, powered by an air compressor, signalling *Bittern* to leave the Great Hall. ROBIN JONES

Above: A4 No. 4464 *Bittern* enters the Great Hall on July 22, 2013.
ROBIN JONES

Right: A steamy arrival: Prince Charles alights from the Royal Train inside the Great Hall of the National Railway Museum, with A4 *Bittern* in the background, around 10.15am on July 22, 2013.
NRM

Below: A rare sight of an engine steaming into the National Railway Museum: *Bittern* stands on the Great Hall turntable at the head of the Royal Train plus support coach.
ROBIN JONES

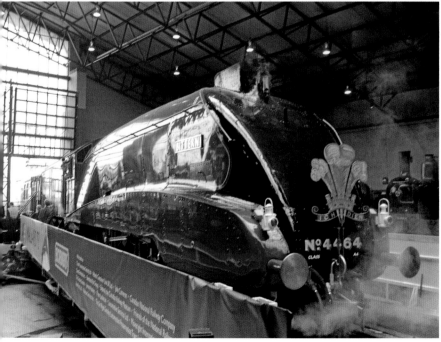

The prince admitted to Sam Dalby, a pupil at St Wilfrid's RC Primary School, that he had liked trains since he was a boy.

Growing up in the final complete decade of steam on the main line, the prince was speaking for a whole generation.

Accompanied by Paul Kirkman in his first official duty since being named National Railway Museum director on a permanent basis, the prince was taken to No. 4468 *Mallard* and boarded the footplate. He sounded *Mallard*'s whistle, powered by an air compressor, to signal for *Bittern* to reverse out of the museum.

He inspected the two repatriated A4s and was shown the digital video recreation of *Mallard*'s 126mph run on Stoke Bank on July 3, 1938, next to the new Mallard Simulator where the public can now experience the thrills of the record-breaking exploits of 75 years ago.

He also spoke to Tobias Lumb, the museum's project manager, who worked on the Mallard 75 celebrations. "He seemed really interested about what the museum was doing," said Tobias.

Afterwards, the prince toured the refurbished Station Hall. He boarded several of the royal carriages including

Left: Accompanied by Lord Crathorne, the prince is introduced to civic dignitaries and police. ROBIN JONES

Left: Moveright International haulier Andrew Goodman (centre), who brought the two North American A4s back to Britain, tells the prince all about it. ROBIN JONES

Far left: The prince begins his tour of the museum with Lord Crathorne, the Lord Lieutenant of North Yorkshire. ROBIN JONES

The prince and National Railway Museum head Paul Kirkman alongside repatriated No. 4489 *Dominion of Canada*. NRM

Left: A self-confessed railway enthusiast since his childhood days: Prince Charles, aged three, stands at the window of the royal saloon and waves to onlookers before the train departs Aberdeen for London on June 16, 1952. NRM

Accompanied by Paul Kirkman, the prince walks up to *Mallard*'s cab steps, with *Bittern* in the background. ROBIN JONES

Left: Roger Canham, executive chairman of Hornby, the headline sponsor of Mallard 75, presents a model to the prince, watched by Helen Ashby, head of knowledge and collections at the museum. Helen gave the prince a copy of the photograph of him on board the Royal Train aged three. NRM

Above: Paul Kirkman explains the finer points of A4 Pacifics to the prince as they walk past *Mallard*. ROBIN JONES

Right: The prince watches a video of the Mallard Simulator digital recreation of the record run of July 3, 1938. ROBIN JONES

Deep in his thoughts on the day: the prince meets the 'other' *Prince William,* former Royal Train Class 47 No. 47798, named after his eldest son. ROBIN JONES

Queen Victoria's favourite carriage, King Edward's saloon and Queen Elizabeth's saloon, used by the royal family during the Second World War.

He then unveiled a plaque to mark the hall's official reopening following a major refurbishment.

Taking time to shake hands with well-wishers outside the public entrance to the museum, he was asked by a bystander whether there was any news from the hospital. He replied: "Absolutely nothing at the moment – we're waiting."

He left by car for York Minister, where he was greeted by the Archbishop of York, Dr John Sentamu. He was shown the new Revealing York Minster exhibition in the cathedral's undercroft, and even tried his hand at stonemasonry with a hammer and chisel among the craftspeople at the Minster Stoneyard, his next engagements on a two-day tour of Yorkshire.

Back in London, crowds gathered, eagerly awaiting news of the royal birth, which happened at 4.24pm.

The Duchess of Cambridge and her baby, accompanied by Prince William, left the hospital the following day. On July 24, the royal baby's name was announced as George Alexander Louis.

Station hall decked out in a manner fit for a prince. NRM

The prince inspects the museum's stupendous collection of vintage Royal Train coaches in Station Hall. NRM

Above: Prince Charles looks out of the window of *Mallard*, just as driver Joe Duddington would have done on his world speed record run on July 3, 1938. ROBIN JONES

Above left: Philip Benham, managing director of the North Yorkshire Moors Railway, home of A4 No. 60007 *Sir Nigel Gresley*, meets the prince. ROBIN JONES

Left: Learning all about repatriated No. 60008 *Dwight D. Eisenhower*. ROBIN JONES

Below: After leaving the museum, the prince spent several minutes chatting to well-wishers outside. ROBIN JONES

The prince unveils a totem-style plaque marking the remodelling of Station Hall towards the end of his museum visit on July 22, 2013. ROBIN JONES

CHAPTER THREE

The ones that got away

The 29 A4s that disappeared with the steam age

IN terms of locomotive preservation, the survival of six streamlined A4 Pacifics means that around a sixth of the class has been saved.

There are many illustrious classes of British steam locomotive rendered extinct, such as the Great Eastern Railway's Claud Hamilton 4-4-0s, the LNWR's Precursor 4-4-0s and the LMS Beyer-Garratt articulated 2-6-0+0-6-2s. Many types passed into oblivion long before the end of steam and modernisation, in an age where there was no official body to preserve priceless historical artefacts for the nation.

The preservation era has seen many new-build groups formed to plug missing gaps in the heritage steam fleet, the most prominent example being A1 Peppercorn Pacific No. 60163 *Tornado*, which took The A1 Steam Locomotive Trust 18 years to achieve, from conception to the main line.

It is unthinkable that *Mallard* might not have been saved, but look at the fate of doyen of the class, No. 2509 *Silver Link*. Despite the key part that it played in British transport history, the Eastern Region sent it to be scrapped at Doncaster rather than sell it, in a classic case of jobsworth intransigence.

Had A4s ended up at Dai Woodham's famous scrapyard at Barry in South Wales, from where 213 ex-British Railways' locomotives were bought for preservation services, we would almost certainly have more, but it was too far from their territory. Dai had a policy of setting aside the steam locomotives for a rainy day while concentrating on the more lucrative business of cutting up redundant wagons. However, he was unique; elsewhere in Britain, locomotives were routinely dismantled often within days of their arrival.

As Barry's catchment area for purchases of scrap locomotives included the south and west of England, Great Western and Southern types were abundantly represented, but there was only one LNER engine saved from there, LNER B1 4-6-0 No. 61264, which in 2014, returned to the main line following its latest overhaul.

Apart from that, LNER types went to scrapyards elsewhere; accordingly, many types that saw service into the Sixties were rendered extinct. Today, we have but one of Gresley's mighty A3 Pacifics in No. 4472 *Flying Scotsman*, and that came about only because the late Alan Pegler bought it from British Railways in 1963; astoundingly, no A3 was set aside for the National Collection. By contrast, thanks to Dai's Barry business plan, 30 Bulleid Pacifics were sold into preservation.

It was not just a case of British Railways realising scrap value without delay. Redundant engines took up siding and works space, without, it seemed at the time, any glimmer of them being used again. There are cases in which it was claimed that they were offered to local councils or museums, but nobody was prepared to give them display space.

The LNER fared worst of all in terms of the preservation of its classes, and in the circumstances we should be immeasurably grateful that we have six A4s today.

Dwight D. Eisenhower and *Dominion of Canada* would also have succumbed to the cutter's torch, had not offers of new homes across the Atlantic been made.

Since the pair were brought back in October 2012, there have been many calls by enthusiasts for them to stay in their country of origin. At least one serious offer has been made to their North American museum owners to buy one, but as has been the case over the past half century, any bids to buy one, or both, have been firmly rebuffed.

Yet these away-from-home museums gave the pair life into preservation meaning they are still in existence and the Great Gatherings of 2013-14 were possible.

It has been said that *Commonwealth of Australia* might also have been similarly saved, but nobody was willing to pay for the transportation costs.

Who would have thought in their wildest dreams that all six survivors might one day be gathered together again – apart from, that is, Steve Davies, the former director of the National Railway Museum.

For a quarter of a century, the A4s flew the flag for British technological excellence, and were the envy of the world.

The achievements of the likes of *Silver Link*, *Mallard*, and *Sir Nigel Gresley*, were the pinnacle of a steam age which had begun in Cornwall with the experiments of Richard Trevithick in the embryonic years of the 19th century.

Appearing as they did towards the end of the Great Depression, they did so much to restore British confidence and pride, especially when *Mallard* snatched the world steam railway speed record from Nazi Germany.

As we stood and admired the six survivors together at York and Shildon, there was universal regret that more examples were not preserved. Here we pay tribute to the 29 A4s that we see no more. The ones that got away.

Below: Twilight years at King's Cross 'Top Shed' in October 1962 just before its closure sees A4 No. 60003 *Andrew K. McCosh,* A3 No. 60044 *Melton* and A4s Nos. 60030 *Golden Fleece* and 60032 *Gannet* lined up. None of these Pacifics made it into preservation. COLOUR-RAIL

No. 60014 *Silver Link* leaves Edinburgh Waverley station in 1958. ERIC TREACY/NRM

An official LNER postcard of No. 2509 *Silver Link,* the locomotive that launched the A4s, setting a new series of speed records on its public trial run.

2509/60014 *SILVER LINK*

SILVER Link was the first A4, the locomotive that began the legend, and it remains unthinkable that all the stops to preserve it for the nation were not pulled out.

Built in 1935 to haul the new streamlined 'Silver Jubilee' train between King's Cross and Newcastle, and outshopped in matching silver and grey livery, No. 2509 was named after a line in a poem by Sir Walter Scott:

"True love's the gift which God has given
To man alone beneath the Heaven.
It is not Fantasy's hot fire,
Whose wishes, soon as granted, fly;
It liveth not in fierce desire,
With dead desire it doth not die:
It is the secret sympathy,

The silver link, the silken tie,
Which heart to heart and mind to mind,
In body and in soul can bind."

Silver Link arrived new 'out of the box' from Doncaster Works at King's Cross on September 13, 1935, and undertook its experimental run on September 27 that year, from King's Cross to Barkston, north of Grantham.

Rarely had the appearance of a new steam locomotive caused so much controversy. Its art deco design was unlike anything else that had been seen before, and those with a fixed mindset about how a steam engine should look hated it. However, the public at large quickly warmed to its radical streamlining.

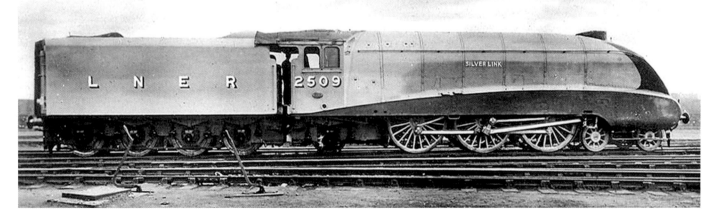

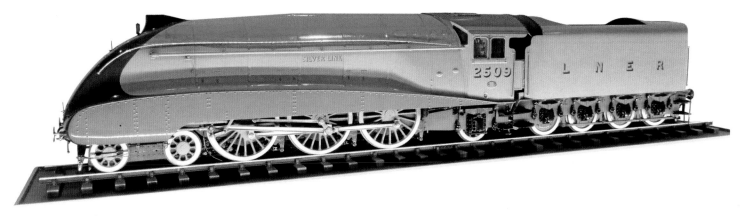

The livery comprised three contrasting shades of grey, the like of which had also never been seen before. The smokebox casing front was dark charcoal grey, while the side skirting and frames were battleship grey and the rest of the engine, the cab and tender were in unlined silver grey. The name was painted on the boiler casing.

On that trial trip, which before the day was out had acquired legendary status, *Silver Link* accelerated to 75mph on the 1-in-200 gradient from Wood Green to Potters Bar.

Its performance thereafter was phenomenal by the standards of the day. It attained 112.5mph down the 1-in-264 gradient from Hitchin, but more astonishingly averaged 107.8mph over the 13.85 miles from Biggleswade to milepost 55.

On this trial trip, staged for publicity purposes, three new world records for any form of railway traction had been established. First, the 25 miles between mileposts 30 and 55 were covered continuously at or above 100mph, and at an average of 107.5mph. Secondly, between Hatfield and Huntingdon, the 41 miles 15 chains were covered at 100.6mph. Thirdly, a 43-mile stretch was covered at an average speed of 100mph continuously.

Also, a new world speed record for steam traction was established, for the average speed of 91.8mph from Wood Green to Fletton Junction.

The feats were achieved, ironically, on the 110th anniversary of the opening of the world's first public steam railway, the Stockton & Darlington. The driver was A J Taylor and the fireman J Luty.

At 10am on October 1, *Silver Link* departed Newcastle Central with the first Up 'Silver Jubilee', and monopolised the service for the next fortnight without any mechanical failures until the second A4 was delivered.

A further three locomotives were built for the 'Silver Jubilee'. The train was booked to run in four hours at a then-amazing average speed of 67.08mph and the initial seven coaches were soon increased to eight because of the train's popularity.

The success of the 'Silver Jubilee' led to an extension of the service to Edinburgh. By 1937, a third service to Leeds & Bradford had been launched. Britain's first inter-city network of fast train services had been born.

Silver Link's new speed records sparked off a period of fierce rivalry between the LNER and LMS over which could get from London to Scotland in the fastest time. The locomotive made a brief appearance in the film *Oh,*

Credit: NRM

Mr. Porter! It was also the subject of art deco posters promoting the 'Silver Jubilee'.

Following the introduction of the LNER's 'Coronation' train in summer 1937, all of the A4s were painted in a uniform garter blue livery. The re-livery saw *Silver Link* and the silver A4s that immediately followed it given nameplates. During the Second World War, *Silver Link* and other A4s were repainted black. At Nationalisation, it became BR No. 60014 and was eventually repainted into green livery.

Allocated to King's Cross throughout its working life, No. 60014 *Silver Link* was an early A4 withdrawal, along with four sister locomotives, on December 29, 1962, as Deltic power superseded steam on the East Coast Main Line.

Holiday camp magnate Billy Butlin made an approach to purchase it, intending to use it as a static exhibit to entertain holidaymakers.

Shamefully, the Eastern Region was unwilling to sell it, preferring to see it scrapped at Doncaster Works, on the same site where it had been built three decades before.

The scrapping of this historic icon was one of the biggest losses to preservation, and is the most glaring absence of all from the Great Gathering. For several years in the heritage era, sister locomotive *Bittern* was painted to represent *Silver Link* in its original silver and grey livery. Two *Silver Link* nameplates are on display in the National Railway Museum, York.

This superb scale model of No. 2509 *Silver Link* is on display in the National Railway Museum at York.
ROBIN JONES

An ignoble end to a locomotive that made history: No. 60014 *Silver Link* at Doncaster Works in March 1965.
PHIL SANGWELL*

No. 60015 *Quicksilver* at King's Cross station on April 29, 1956.
MJ READE/COLOUR-RAIL

2510/60015 *QUICKSILVER*

Making its debut in service on September 21, 1935, was No. 2510 *Quicksilver*, the second of the A4s to be built.

It was delivered from Doncaster a fortnight after *Silver Link*.

The first four A4s were all painted in shades of silver and grey.

Quicksilver was also shedded at King's Cross, apart from a short period at Grantham in the early 1950s.

As No. 60015, it was withdrawn from King's Cross 'Top Shed' on April 25, 1963, just before the shed closed.

No. 60016 *Silver King*, by then long having been repainted into BR green, heads a rake of Gresley teak coaches in BR maroon and cream livery at York on July 1, 1959.
COLOUR-RAIL

2511/60016 *SILVER KING*

The only one of the four silver A4s to be allocated to Gateshead, entering service on November 5, 1935, No. 2511 *Silver King* worked the 'Silver Jubilee' only when one of the King's Cross allocation failed in the north-east.

However, it worked more regular express passenger trains than any other A4 in the early years of the class. It hauled the daily 11.10am Down express from Newcastle to Edinburgh non stop, returning at 5.15pm.

The last survivor of the initial four engines, it was withdrawn at Aberdeen Ferryhill on March 19, 1965.

A LNER postcard view of *Silver King* in its original livery.

2512/60017 *SILVER FOX*

No. 2512 *Silver Fox* was the fourth of the silver A4s, entering service on December 18, 1935, and allocated to King's Cross.

It carried a stainless steel silver fox emblem on each side, supplied by steel manufacturer Samuel Fox Ltd.

Silver Fox was the subject on another A4 trial run, on August 27, 1936.

Chosen because it was the newest member of the class, it was driven by *Silver Link*'s George Henry Haygreen on a normal fare-paying service intended to measure water and coal consumption, and to beat *Silver Link*'s 112mph record into the bargain.

Although Haygreen was never told that a record attempt was expected, and therefore he did not gain sufficient speed on the climb of Stoke Bank; despite the lack of a sufficient reserve of boiler pressure, 113mph was attained with a total load of 270 tons including the dynamometer car.

The figure is widely accepted as an official British record for a revenue-earning steam train, but the middle big end sustained damage.

The train arrived into King's Cross seven minutes late. Going back, *Silver Link* took over and arrived four minutes early.

The conclusion drawn from the test run was that the A4s had a reserve of power and could haul 10 coaches on a planned service from Glasgow to London.

No. 60017 plays a prominent role in the 1954 British Transport Film Elizabethan Express which follows the revival of non-stop London to Edinburgh runs and features footage of the water trough and corridor tender in use.

Following experiments in the 1950s, it was decided in 1957 to equip all the single-chimney A4s with Kylchap double blastpipes and chimneys. *Silver Fox* was the first to be fitted under this plan.

After a short spell at New England after the closure of King's Cross 'Top Shed', No. 60017 was withdrawn on October 20, 1963.

No. 60017 *Silver Fox* at King's Cross, about 1960, preparing to haul the 'Tees-Tyne Pullman' to Darlington. NRM

No. 60017 *Silver Fox* leaving Welwyn South Tunnel on the Down 'Tees-Tyne Pullman' in 1955. NRM

4462/60004 *WILLIAM WHITELAW*

No. 4462 entered traffic on August 30, 1937, and was originally named *Great Snipe*. While the first four A4s were all painted silver and grey to mark the silver jubilee of George V, the rest of the class were intended to be named after flying birds.

Most of the final batch of A4s, all of which entered service in garter blue livery but were not fitted with a corridor tender, soon received names of high-ranking LNER officials, this one becoming *William Whitelaw*, after the company's chairman, from July 1941.

After being renamed, it was transferred to Haymarket and equipped with a corridor tender so it could work the non-stop runs from King's Cross to Edinburgh. It spent the rest of its working life in Scotland.

After the outbreak of the Second World War, it was decided to remove the skirting of the A4s from both behind and in front of the cylinders to speed up maintenance. No. 4462 was the first to have the skirting removed, in June 1941, but re-entered traffic a month later with a modified form of skirting in front of the cylinders. This arrangement lasted until July 1942 when, in common with all other A4s, all the skirtings had been removed.

It was one of the more widely travelled A4s, seeing periods at King's Cross, Gateshead and Haymarket before withdrawal as No. 60004 from Ferryhill on July 17, 1966.

No. 60004 *William Whitelaw* is seen leaving Berwick-on-Tweed for London in 1952, in a photograph by the late Bishop, Eric Treacy. He was often allowed special access to many areas denied to other railway photographers. He also befriended many of the footplate crews, occasionally persuading them to create special smoke effects for the camera. NRM

A 1937 edition of the Baedeker guide.

4469 *GADWALL/SIR RALPH WEDGWOOD*

No. 4469 *Gadwall* entered traffic on August 30, 1938, and was renamed *Sir Ralph Wedgwood* after the man who had been the chief officer of the LNER for 16 years.

Sadly, No. 4469 would not last anywhere near that time in service, for it ended up being destroyed in a Nazi bombing raid.

Allocated to Gateshead shed throughout its short life, No. 4469 suffered a direct hit from a Luftwaffe bomber on April 29, 1942, along with B16 4-6-0 No. 925, as they stood in York North shed.

The East Coast Main Line and its centres of engineering and communications like York were prime targets between 1940 and 1943.

York suffered its worst air raid of the war beginning at 2.30am. The attack followed in the immediate wake of Luftwaffe raids on two other cathedral cities, Norwich and Bath, and an earlier one on Exeter.

These attacks became named the Baedeker raids, because it was believed that Hitler, furious at the RAF's attacks on Lübeck and Rostock, took a Baedeker tourist guidebook and demanded that every historic place in England marked with three stars be bombed in retaliation.

More than 70 German planes – Junkers, Heinkels and Dorniers – were involved in the York raid. The crews dive-bombed city streets, strafing them

with machine-gun fire in a bid to destroy the morale of the population. The railway line, the station, the carriage works and the airfield were also hit, but York Minster escaped.

The raid ended 90 minutes after it began, leaving 92 people dead and hundreds injured. Houses and schools were destroyed, schools wrecked and the Guildhall and St Martin-le-Grand church in Coney Street were burned out.

Yet York people went back to work the same day. *The Daily Mail* reported: "The gates of York still stand high, like the spirit of its people who, after nearly two hours of intense bombing and machine gunning, were clearing up today."

No. 4469, which by the time of the attack had been repainted into NE wartime black livery, and No. 925 were scrapped. The name *Sir Ralph Wedgwood* was afterwards transferred to No. 4466 *Herring Gull*, while the tiny LNER Y8 0-4-0T No. 8091 (NER 560) got its chime whistle.

In October 1999, *Heritage Railway* reported that Sheffield Railwayana Auctions had been approached by a man who had found a bent nameplate from the bombed locomotive in the garden tool shed of a house near York and wanted to know its value, but nothing more was heard.

Right: No. 4469 lies damaged beyond repair in the wreckage of York North locomotive depot. NRM

Far right: A plaque marking the exact spot where *Sir Ralph Wedgwood* was destroyed was placed inside the Great Hall of the National Railway Museum by the Gresley Society on April 29, 1992, the 50th anniversary of the raid. NRM

LNER

ON THIS TRACK THE LNER STREAMLINE PACIFIC LOCOMOTIVE SIR RALPH WEDGWOOD WAS DESTROYED DURING AN AIR RAID ON THE NIGHT OF 28/29 APRIL 1942 NEARBY CLASS B16 No. 925 WAS ALSO DESTROYED

THIS PLAQUE WAS PLACED IN REMEMBRANCE BY THE GRESLEY SOCIETY ON THE FIFTIETH ANNIVERSARY 29 APRIL 1992

4482 *GOLDEN EAGLE*/60023

No. 4482 *Golden Eagle* was the first of the second batch of A4s. These 17, Nos. 4482-98, were intended to be painted in LNER standard passenger apple green livery, with black and white lining and gold figures and letters with red shading and named after birds. They were intended to haul standard LNER varnished teak coaching stock.

As it happened, only Nos. 4482-87 and 4493-95 appeared in this livery.

No. 4482 entered service on December 22, 1936, and, like the rest of the A4s, was repainted into LNER garter blue, in January 1938.

On June 30, 1963, *Golden Eagle* hauled the Railway Correspondence & Travel Society's 'Three Summits Tour' from Leeds to Carlisle. It ran the 40.9 miles from Mallerstang signalbox to Cumwhinton in 31 minutes 17 seconds; the average speed of 78mph is believed to be a steam record for this section.

It had an unusual allocation history, spending time at King's Cross, Haymarket and Gateshead before ending up

at Aberdeen Ferryhill from where it was withdrawn on October 30, 1964.

Its latter-day duties included the three-hour expresses to Glasgow Buchanan Street.

4483 *KINGFISHER*/60024

No. 4483 *Kingfisher* entered traffic on Boxing Day 1936 and spent virtually all its working life based in Scotland working from Haymarket until transferring to Aberdeen Ferryhill for the Glasgow expresses. It did, however, have brief spells at King's Cross and Doncaster before the Second World War.

In October 1954, plaques of the badge of *HMS Kingfisher* were fitted on either side of the boiler casing.

It was withdrawn on September 5, 1966 after working the Scottish Region's A4 farewell railtour, the last of the class in common use.

However, due to a shortage of motive power available at the depot on September 14, 1966, Kingfisher worked the 8.24am Glasgow to Aberdeen return trip which heralded the final revenue-earning service for an A4.

It was outlasted in BR service only by No. 60019 *Bittern*.

An initial bid to preserve it was made, but the plans foundered when it was discovered that the locomotive had firebox problems.

It was cut up by scrap merchant Hughes Bolckow of Blyth in early 1967.

No. 60024 *Kingfisher* is pictured heading 'The Elizabethan' at Edinburgh Waverley station, with a 9.45am departure for King's Cross, in 1961. ERIC TREACY/NRM

4484/60025 FALCON

Although No. 4484 *Falcon*, which entered traffic on January 23, 1937, was initially a Haymarket engine, it was associated with King's Cross for most of its working life.

Through its years in service, it was equipped with a corridor tender.

It was one of those that survived the closure of 'Top Shed' to see a brief spell at Peterborough's New England depot, from where, as No. 60025, it was withdrawn on October 20, 1963, bringing an end to A4 operation on the Eastern Region.

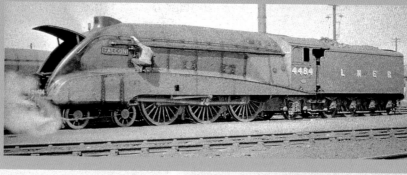

Above right: From near the dawn of colour photography, this view of No. 4484 in the garter blue into which it was repainted in December 1937 livery was taken at Haymarket in August 1938. COLOUR-RAIL

Right: No. 60025 *Falcon* is seen heading the 'Tees-Tyne Pullman' at Grantham on July 4, 1956. DC OVENDEN/NRM

4485 KESTREL/60026

No. 4485 *Kestrel* continued the bird theme, and again started life at Haymarket after entering traffic March 20, 1937. However, November 1, 1947 saw the renaming of the engine as *Miles Beevor* after the acting chief general manager of the LNER. Beevor, an Oxford graduate, solicitor, Hertfordshire JP and RAF Flight Lieutenant and chief legal advisor to the LNER in 1943, later served as chief secretary and legal advisor for the British Transport Commission between 1947 and 1951.

From 1954-58, he was managing director of Brush Group Ltd, which produced diesel locomotives following the 1955 BR Modernisation Plan. He died on September 9, 1994 aged 94.

As No. 60026, the locomotive from September 1949 until January 1953, carried dark blue BR livery with black

and white lining and was associated with the Eastern Region, working from King's Cross and Grantham sheds, before finishing its days back in Scotland as one of Ferryhill's allocation until withdrawal on December 21, 1965.

Parts of the locomotive were to live on after scrapping. No. 60026 was moved to Crewe Works after withdrawal, to provide spare parts including driving wheels, for preserved No. 60007 *Sir Nigel Gresley*. In 1967, both No. 60007 and No. 60010 *Dominion of Canada* were in the works being prepared for preservation and No. 60026 stood outside as a source for spare parts.

The driving wheels of No. 60007 were damaged beyond economical repair, although advances in technology would mean that today they could have

No. 60026 *Miles Beevor* on shed at Grantham in March 1959. COLOUR-RAIL

4486 *MERLIN*/60027

No. 4486 *Merlin* started life at Haymarket after entering service on March 13, 1937. It hauled the nine-coach 'Coronation' – the second LNER high-speed train – which was launched on July 3 that year, running from King's Cross to Edinburgh.

The train, including the observation car, was painted in a two-tone blue livery.

Merlin, a highly regarded Edinburgh A4, throughout its career, also worked 'The Elizabethan' in BR days.

Always based in Scotland, it also had a period at Edinburgh's other North British shed at St Margaret's before becoming one of two A4s working from the Caledonian shed at St Rollox, Glasgow.

As No. 60027, it carried an *HMS Merlin* plaque on the side.

It was withdrawn on September 3, 1965.

No. 60027 *Merlin* is seen heading through Potters Bar in September 1959.
J JARVIS/COLOUR-RAIL

4487 *SEA EAGLE*/60028 *WALTER K WHIGHAM*

Entering traffic on March 20, 1937, No. 4487 *Sea Eagle* was initially a Gateshead engine but became one of the long-term King's Cross allocations.

It was renamed after Walter K. Whigham, an LNER director, in October 1947.

During the summer of 1948, BR attempted to restart the non-stop services that were cancelled at the outbreak of the Second World War.

In August 1948, serious flooding caused the collapse of several bridges and culverts on the East Coast Main Line in south-east Scotland, with many diverted via Selby and Leeds and over the Settle-Carlisle line. From August 24, the non-stop A4 run was diverted over the Waverley route to St Boswells, then via Kelso to Tweedmouth to rejoin the main line.

On this first run, *Walter K. Whigham* ran non-stop from Edinburgh to King's Cross via St Boswells, setting a new a distance record of 408.65 miles. The locomotive repeated the feat on the southbound run the same day and on the northbound run on August 26.

In 1949, the 'Capitals Express' was also reinstated, and after being accelerated, was renamed 'The Elizabethan' in 1953, marking the accession of the Queen to the throne. This train ran for three months each year, in the summer only, and the set of 11 coaches was that used by the 'Flying

Scotsman' train for the rest of the year augmented, as necessary, at busy periods.

Walter K. Whigham hauled the first 'Elizabethan' train on June 29, 1953. In June 1961, it hauled the Royal Train. That summer marked the end of steam on 'The Elizabethan'. However, it was withdrawn on December 29, 1962.

No. 60028 *Walter K. Whigham* heads 'The Elizabethan' in BR days.
NRM

No. 60028 *Walter K. Whigham* heads an Up Newcastle express out of Welwyn Tunnel on June 2, 1951.
BEN BROOKSBANK*

No. 4487 *Sea Eagle* is shown passing along the cliff tops north of Berwick-upon-Tweed with the 'Flying Scotsman' named train 1938. The train included a three-coach restaurant car, also known as a 'triplet'. NRM

No. 60011 *Empire of India* at Aberdeen Ferryhill in June 1962.
COLOUR-RAIL

4490 *EMPIRE OF INDIA*/60011

Making its first appearance on June 25, 1937, No. 4490 *Empire of India* was initially one of the five King's Cross engines designated to haul the high-speed 'Coronation' train.

The 'Imperial' five were named after territories of the British Empire. They were all painted in a garter blue livery to match the carriages, and had cut-out metal numbers and plaques bearing coats of arms of the countries after which they were named fitted beneath the cabside running numbers.

Only King's Cross and Haymarket engines were rostered for the non-stop train.

No. 4490 was transferred to Haymarket in March 1938. It remained there until it was transferred in June 1962 to Ferryhill, from where it was withdrawn on May 11, 1964.

Right: No. 60012 *Commonwealth of Australia* backs on to an express train at Newcastle station in the mid-1950s. ERIC TREACY/NRM

Below: An official LNER postcard view of No. 4491 *Commonwealth of Australia* as new.

4491 *COMMONWEALTH OF AUSTRALIA*/60012

No. 4491 *Commonwealth of Australia* was a Haymarket engine and worked the inaugural Up 'Coronation' on July 3, 1937, having entered traffic on June 22.

Like other Haymarket engines, it also worked to Dundee, Aberdeen and Glasgow, and regularly hauled 'The Elizabethan'.

It was withdrawn from Ferryhill on August 20, 1964 and cut up in 1965 by Motherwell Machinery & Scrap, Wishaw.

4492 *DOMINION OF NEW ZEALAND*/60013

No. 4492 *Dominion of New Zealand* the last of the five 'Imperial' A4s, entered service on June 27, 1937 and hauled the inaugural Up 'West Riding Limited' on September 27 that year.

It carried a whistle from New Zealand Railways which was bigger and pitched lower than the standard chime whistle and was allocated to King's Cross throughout until withdrawal on April 18, 1963. It was one of 13 A4s, including *Sir Ralph Wedgwood*, which were scrapped at Doncaster Works.

In recent times, *Bittern* briefly masqueraded on the main line as No. 4492, before reverting to its correct identity but still in its 1930s livery.

4493 *WOODCOCK*/60029

Entering service on July 26, 1937, No. 4493 was given the name *Woodcock* that had been briefly carried by No. 4489.

In 1948, after Nationalisation, it was one of four A4s briefly given purple livery, as BR experimented with different liveries.

Initially a Gateshead engine, it spent most of its life at King's Cross, withdrawn on October 20, 1963 after six months at New England.

No. 60029 *Woodcock* is seen billowing smoke as it leaves Copenhagen Tunnel near King's Cross station with a Newcastle-bound express passenger train in 1954.
ERIC TREACY/NRM

4494 *OSPREY*/60003 *ANDREW K. McCOSH*

The last of the apple green A4s, No. 4494 entered service on August 12, 1937, named *Osprey*. It was renamed after LNER director Andrew K. McCosh in October 1942.

The haphazard system of renumbering by the LNER after the Second World War, which was perpetuated by BR, is reflected in the fact that this locomotive became No. 3 and therefore No. 60003.

It started life at Heaton but was a King's Cross engine for most of its working life, being withdrawn on December 29, 1962.

No. 60003 *Andrew K. McCosh* exits Hadley North tunnel with the Down 'Yorkshire Pullman' in 1953. This heavy train comprised 11 Pullman cars with portions for Hull (detached at Doncaster), Bradford and Harrogate, which split at Leeds. NRM

4495 *GREAT SNIPE*/60030 *GOLDEN FLEECE*

Entering service on August 30, 1937, No. 4495 *Great Snipe* soon became the first of two engines designated for the 'West Riding Limited', the other being No. 4496 *Golden Shuttle* (later *Dwight D. Eisenhower*).

Accordingly, *Great Snipe* was almost immediately renamed *Golden Fleece* and repainted from green into garter blue in recognition of the West Riding's wool industry.

This eight-coach train was scheduled to run from King's Cross to Bradford and Leeds in two hours 44 minutes, an average of 67.9mph. The locomotive was withdrawn on December 29, 1962.

No. 60031 *Golden Plover* prepares to head 'The Elizabethan' to the right of Peppercorn A1 Pacific No. 60158 *Aberdonian*, departing from King's Cross.

SCOTLAND FOR YOUR HOLIDAYS

Scotland For Your Holidays: this Terence Cuneo BR poster from 1952 depicts *Golden Plover* crossing the Forth Bridge in Scotland. Cuneo withstood gales of more than 50mph to sketch this scene from a girder high above the track. He recounted: "Working conditions here were frankly terrifying. Although swaddled in a flying suit, duffel coat, balaclava and mittens, to say nothing of long woollen underwear – I was frozen!" NRM

4497 *GOLDEN PLOVER*/60031

Combining the 'golden' and 'bird' naming themes, No. 4497 *Golden Plover* entered traffic on October 2, 1937, and was a Haymarket engine for virtually all of its life.

In the Thirties, it hauled 39 consecutive 'Coronation' round trips.

It became the second A4 allocated to St Rollox in February 1962, primarily for Glasgow-Aberdeen expresses. No. 60031 was withdrawn in 1965.

No. 60018 *Sparrow Hawk* is seen departing northbound from York in 1961. M CHAPMAN/COLOUR-RAIL

4463 *SPARROW HAWK*/60018

No. 4463 *Sparrow Hawk* spent its entire career as a Gateshead or Heaton engine, until withdrawal as No. 60018 on June 19, 1963.

4465 *GUILLEMOT*/60020

No. 4465 *Guillemot* was a Gateshead locomotive throughout from January 8, 1938 until withdrawal on March 20, 1964.

No. 60020 *Guillemot* departs southbound from York on March 17, 1957.

4466 *HERRING GULL*/60006 *SIR RALPH WEDGWOOD*

No. 4466 *Herring Gull* was a King's Cross engine, taking the identity of the bombed A4 and renamed *Sir Ralph Wedgwood* from January 1944.

After a period at Grantham it returned to King's Cross. When 'Top Shed' closed in June 1963, No. 60006 was transferred to St Margaret's and then Aberdeen Ferryhill, from where it was withdrawn on September 3, 1965.

While they were designed for Britain's fastest express passenger trains, A4s also took their turn on freight, especially in the latter years. No. 60006 *Sir Ralph Wedgwood* heads through St Neots with a train of box vans on July 20, 1961. K FAIREY/COLOUR-RAIL

No. 60021 *Wild Swan* in action near Selby. E SANDERSON/ COLOUR-RAIL

4467 *WILD SWAN*/60021

No. 4467 *Wild Swan* was always associated with the southern section of the East Coast Main Line, allocated mainly to King's Cross apart from a spell at Doncaster.

It was withdrawn from New England on October 20, 1963.

4499 *POCHARD*/60002 *SIR MURROUGH WILSON*

The LNER numbering system became particularly haphazard with No. 4499 *Pochard*, although a partial semblance of order was introduced by Edward Thompson's renumbering system. Those A4s named after directors and other dignitaries became Nos. 1-8, the 'Commonwealth' names Nos. 9-13 and silver names Nos. 14-17, followed by an assortment of birds and others.

Pochard was renamed after Sir Murrough Wilson, deputy chairman of the LNER and given stainless steel cut out numbers and letters in April 1939, as No. 2, and therefore later as BR No. 60002.

A Gateshead engine throughout its life, apart from a few weeks in 1943 when it was based at King's Cross, it was withdrawn on May 4, 1964.

No. 4499 *Pochard* hauls the Down 'Yorkshire Pullman' from King's Cross to Bradford, Harrogate and Hull in the 1930s. The locomotive on the left was the first large-boiler 4-4-2 of the GNR, now preserved at the National Railway Museum. NRM

4500 *GARGANEY*/60001 *SIR RONALD MATTHEWS*

No. 4500 *Garganey* was the first A4 to be renamed after a high-ranking LNER official. It became No. 1 *Sir Ronald Matthews* in March 1939, and after Nationalisation, BR No. 60001.

A Gateshead engine throughout, it was withdrawn on October 12, 1964, one the last A4s to operate south of the border.

No. 60001 *Sir Ronald Matthews* at Grantham shed. PJ HUGHES/ COLOUR-RAIL

No. 60032 *Gannet* heads the 'Heart of Midlothian' at Hadley Wood in May 1960. COLOUR-RAIL

4900 *GANNET*/60032

Entering traffic on May 17, 1938, No. 4900 *Gannet* retained its name throughout.

It became an Eastern Region engine, based first at Doncaster, then King's Cross and finishing its days at New England on October 20, 1963.

No. 60005 *Sir Charles Newton* heads through Chaloners Whin southbound from York on August 4, 1957. COLOUR-RAIL

4901 *CAPERCAILLIE*/60005 *SIR CHARLES NEWTON*

No. 4901 *Capercaillie* was one of the A4s fitted with the double Kylchap blastpipe and chimney from new, and one of the last three of the class to be built.

The outbreak of the Second World War, followed by the death of Sir Nigel Gresley in 1941, meant many existing A4s were not given these modifications until the Fifties.

Capercaillie was renamed *Charles H. Newton* in September 1942 and *Sir Charles Newton* in June 1943.

This locomotive once hauled a 21-coach train weighing 730 tonnes over 25 miles at an average speed of 75.9mph.

Based at Gateshead throughout its working life until the final few months when it was transferred to Scotland, first allocated to St Margaret's, and withdrawn from Aberdeen Ferryhill on March 12, 1964.

4902 *SEAGULL*/60033

No. 4902 *Seagull*, one of the final three A4s to be built, was another engine fitted from the outset with a Kylchap double blastpipe and chimney.

Allocated to King's Cross throughout its working life, *Seagull* was chosen to take part in the 1948 Locomotive Exchanges.

The newly formed British Railways had inherited an arbitrary collection of locomotives from the 'Big Four' companies and with the ultimate goal of standardisation, wanted to find which locomotive types could perform well in other regions.

Mallard was chosen to represent the new Eastern Region because of its double chimney, but failed on April 28, to be replaced by *Seagull*.

Seagull complete dynamometer car trials on the Western Region, making the first visits by an A4 to Plymouth.

It struggled up the infamous 1-in-40 South Devon banks at less than 20mph, but showed on the run from Exeter to Taunton, it was the equivalent of a GWR Castle 4-6-0, taking the run to Castle Cary at an impressive 75mph.

However, *Seagull* failed at an early stage while undertaking similar runs on the Southern Region, breaking down while heading an 'Atlantic Coast Express' to Exeter… and was replaced by *Mallard*.

The story was not yet over, for *Mallard* failed on the Southern, and was again substituted by *Seagull*, which completed two dynamometer car trials.

It was withdrawn on December 29, 1962.

No. 60033 *Seagull* arriving at Paddington during the 1948 Locomotive Exchanges. COLOUR-RAIL

No. 60034 *Lord Faringdon* passes Westwood Junction signalbox at Peterborough with the Up 'Flying Scotsman' train on August 15, 1959. On the right are the great New England west and east yards and beyond, in the distance, stands the large water tower and coaling plant of New England shed, where several A4s were briefly shedded in the mid-1960s. BEN BROOKSBANK*

4903 PEREGRINE/60034 *LORD FARINGDON*

No. 4903 *Peregrine* was the 35th and last A4 to be built, entering service on July 1, 1938 at Doncaster.

Renamed *Lord Faringdon* by BR in March 1948, following the scrapping of a Great Central Railway 4-6-0 of the same name, it was also the final A4 to carry the LNER garter blue livery, which it did with British Railways on the tender.

It was repainted into BR dark green in August 1952.

No. 60034 also took part in the 1948 Locomotive Exchanges, in its case on the King's Cross to Leeds route in April that year and LMR's Euston to Carlisle route in May.

When King's Cross 'Top Shed' closed in June 1963, No. 60034 was at first transferred to St Margaret's, but was soon reallocated to Ferryhill fleet from where it was withdrawn as No. 60034, numerically the last in the BR series, on August 24, 1966.

Driver Bill Hoole and his fireman lean from the cab of No. 60034 *Lord Faringdon* to consult with the guard, before the departure of the 9.50am Leeds Central to King's Cross service in 1956. ERIC TREACY/NRM

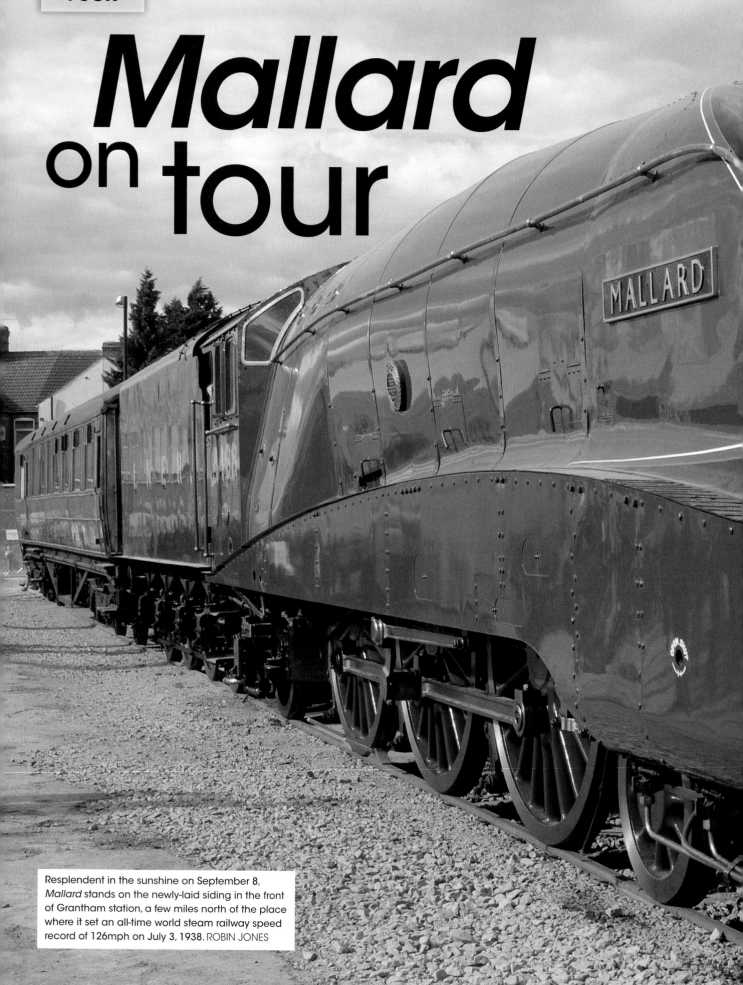

CHAPTER FOUR

Mallard on tour

Resplendent in the sunshine on September 8, *Mallard* stands on the newly-laid siding in the front of Grantham station, a few miles north of the place where it set an all-time world steam railway speed record of 126mph on July 3, 1938. ROBIN JONES

Just over 65 years earlier, livery in June 1948, another blue A4 was photographed at Grantham, in the form of No. 60028 *Walter K. Whigham*.
COLOUR-RAIL

Coupled behind *Mallard* at Grantham was classic LNER teak buffer car No. 641. Built at York coach works for fast Liverpool Street to Cambridge trains, the typical Thirties-style interior layout consisted of a kitchen at one end and an open saloon with two plus one seating for 24 passengers and bar counter area in the centre of coach. No. 641, by then carrying the Inter City blue and grey livery was withdrawn from main line service in 1972. It was sold to the Dart Valley Railway and cosmetically restored at Swindon Works. However, this work merely masked bigger problems which led to its continual deterioration. After the Dart Valley decided it was beyond economic repair, LNER Coach Association members Dave Cullingworth and Paul Denston bought it and moved it to North Yorkshire. Finally, after a protracted and painstakingly thorough rebuild, No. 641 was presented to the North Yorkshire Moors Railway in 1994.
ROBIN JONES

In the weeks that followed the phenomenally-successful first Great Gathering, No. 4468 *Mallard* went on an East Midlands-oriented tour of its own to mark the 75th anniversary of its 126mph world record-breaking run.

Despite the fact that it was purely on static display, having not steamed since its 50th anniversary celebrations in 1988, the public response was again astonishing.

The first stop was Grantham station, which stands just north of the stretch of Stoke Bank, the legendary gradient of the East Coast Main Line down which *Mallard's* and many other speed records were both set and broken.

Mallard had not passed through the Lincolnshire town for more than half a century. However, a special weekend festival at the station was arranged in its honour on September 7-8, 2013. Sponsored by Mortons Media Group, the publisher of *The Railway*

Magazine, Heritage Railway and *Rail Express*, the event was organised by South Kesteven District Council under the banner of the Mallard Grantham Partnership.

The festival ground was based around a siding specially relaid to the immediate south of the main station front, and behind the public car park, by contractor Carillion.

Devon & Cornwall Railways Class 56 No. 56311 towed *Mallard* and one of its ECML successors, Class 55 Deltic No. 55019 *Royal Highland Fusilier*, from York to Grantham, as a small crowd gathered at the city's station to watch the convoy depart on September 4.

Entrance to the two-day Story of Speed festival, which also incorporated a host of ancillary events around the town, was free.

The event from packed from opening time on the Saturday to closing time on the Sunday, with up to the last minute, lengthy queues of families forming to board *Mallard's* footplate.

From start to finish, people were jostling to have their picture taken in the sunshine with the celebrity engine as a backdrop.

The attendance, however, vastly exceeded all expectations, with more than 15,000 turning up over the two days – a figure of which any operational railway gala would have been proud.

On the Saturday evening, a talk entitled The Quest for Speed on Rail took place with Dr Alfred Gottwaldt, senior curator, railways, from the Berlin Technical Museum and Bob Gwynne, the NRM's associate curator of Rail Vehicles, chaired by Nick Pigott, editor of *The Railway Magazine*, and a native of Grantham. Dr Gottwaldt spoke about the German 'Flying Hamburger' – the ground-breaking two-car diesel railcar set which prompted the LNER and Gresley to show that steam could do better, and which therefore provided an impetus for the design of the streamlined A4s.

On the Sunday, Nick Pigott unveiled a Grantham Civic Society information signboard

Approaching Grantham on September 4, *Mallard* passes the landmark of the town's St Wulfram's Church for the first time since 1962. BRIAN SHARPE

En route from the National Railway Museum at York to Grantham, No. 4468 is towed through Saxilby station by Devon & Cornwall Railways Class 56 No. 56311 on September 4. BRIAN SHARPE

Stunning from any angle: *Mallard* stands on the specially-relaid siding at Grantham station, with Deltic No. 55019 *Royal Highland Fusilier* behind and Devon & Cornwall Railways Class 56 No. 56311, which towed the pair from York. ROBIN JONES

Mallard
The Story of Speed

In 1938, rail history was made near Grantham.

The world's fastest steam locomotive returns in the Story of Speed Festival, Grantham Railway Station, September 7-8, 2013

Souvenir programme £1

A never-ending stream of visitors clamouring to photograph the record breaker at Freightliner on September 15. SHAUN FLANNERY/DBC

on Platform 1 beneath the station sign and looking south in the direction of *Mallard's* record-breaking great journey.

Organisers were amazed at the public response to the festival, which prompted talk of a repeat. Spokesman Henry Cleary said: "People have been responding to the beauty of the engine, as well as its history.

"The town has a wonderful engineering heritage. People are tremendously proud of Sir Nigel Gresley, who designed *Mallard*, and his achievements.

"What's been fun is that so many locomotive drivers pulling into their station have been sounding their horns as a salute to *Mallard.*"

He said that the festival generated a very high profile for Grantham in media interest, while the relaying of the siding cleared an eyesore site at the station which forms part of the 'gateway' to the town.

He added: "There is real potential to capture some of the momentum generated for the future and we should learn from all aspects of this first time event and how it might be sustained and improved."

The following Thursday, September 13, *Mallard* was taken back to its Doncaster Works erecting shop birthplace, possibly for the last time ever.

There, it broke a banner as it was pushed back out into the daylight in front of 100 ticketed guests and VIPs.

That symbolic relaunch preceded a gala dinner in Doncaster's historic Georgian Mansion House attended by dignitaries including Tim Godfrey, grandson of Sir Nigel Gresley.

During the following weekend, September 15-16, *Mallard* was displayed at the Freightliner Ltd Railport in Doncaster, with admission again free. Its appearance deliberately coincided with Doncaster's St Leger Festival Week, echoing the

words of world steam speed record-setting driver Joe Duddington. "She couldn't have done better in the St Leger," he said afterwards.

Retired amateur jockey Clare Balding presented Channel 4 coverage of the festival live from *Mallard's* footplate on the Saturday morning.

Around 2500 members of the public attended the weekend event at Railport, considerably fewer than the number who turned up at Grantham.

Organisers said that this may have been due to the fact that Railport is not immediately accessible from the town centre.

FirstGroup laid on shuttle buses for the event to ferry visitors from the station to the Freightliner depot every 10 to 15 minutes, their headboards reading '4468 Mallard.' On the Sunday morning, two of the buses with the special destination boards were lined up alongside the A4.

Above: *Mallard* stands outside the erecting shop at The Plant possibly for the last time. Doncaster Works was established by the Great Northern Railway in 1853, replacing the previous workshops in Boston and Peterborough. Until 1867 it only undertook repairs and maintenance. Among the ground-breaking locomotives the works produced were the Stirling Singles, the Ivatt Atlantics and the Gresley Pacifics, including A1/A3 No. 4472 *Flying Scotsman*, and the A4s.

In 1957, the last of more than 2000 steam locomotives was built and, in 1962, carriage building at Doncaster also finished, but the works was modernised with the addition of a diesel locomotive repair shop. Under British Rail Engineering, new diesel shunters and 25kV electric locomotives were built, along with Class 56 and Class 58 diesel-electric locomotives. In early 2008 the main locomotive repair shop was demolished to make way for housing. BRIAN SHARPE

Left: On Thursday, September 12, in front of a select audience of people who had paid £100 for a celebratory meal at the Mansion House in Doncaster, No. 4468 *Mallard* emerges from the erecting shop at Doncaster works where it was outshopped on March 3, 1938. BRIAN SHARPE

The destination boards on this pair of FirstGroup buses which ran shuttle services from Doncaster station to the Freightliner Yard indicate the purpose of their journey. PETER MAIR

Mallard outside the former Staveley Midland roundhouse, once part of the empire of the LNER's great rival the LMS, and now Britain's only rail-connected roundhouse. ROBIN JONES

Plans are afoot to install a stained glass window at Grantham station marking *Mallard's* world record feat. Artist Michael Brown and his son Tom have been given the green light by Network Rail and East Coast following six months of negotiations, and hope to complete the window by the end of 2014, but first need to raise £800 through public donations. More details are available at www.kickstarter.com MICHAEL BROWN

Anthony Coulls, the NRM's senior curator of railway vehicles, said: "During *Mallard's* big anniversary year we wanted to give the people of Doncaster the chance to see the world's fastest steam locomotive in the town where it was built."

After its appearance at Doncaster, *Mallard* was taken to Chesterfield for the Barrow Hill Live 2013! event which was held at the former Staveley Midland roundhouse on September 28-29.

The model-oriented event, sponsored by both Bachmann and Hornby, celebrated 160 years of

Doncaster Works by bringing together a range of steam and diesel locomotives that all have an association with the plant.

Mallard was lined up alongside new-build Peppercorn A1 Pacific No. 60163 *Tornado*, which was celebrating its fifth anniversary of moving for the first time.

Following the conclusion of Barrow Hill Live! No. 56301 towed *Mallard* back to its York home, where its connecting rods were refitted, in readiness for its appearance in the second line-up of all six surviving A4s at the autumn Great Gathering. ∎

Also on show at Barrow Hill Live! was another but more recent bird-named veteran of the East Coast Main Line, the prototype Crewe, 1986-built Class 89 6000bhp Co-Co electric locomotive, No. 89001, officially named *Avocet* by Prime Minister Margaret Thatcher on January 16, 1989, at Sandy – the home of the Royal Society for the Protection of Birds, whose logo is an Avocet. Sadly, its success was at the opposite end of the spectrum from the A4s. Designed by Brush Traction to meet a British Rail specification, the requirements were subsequently changed, but not before the Loughborough company committed to build the prototype locomotive. Its locomotive was used on passenger trains from Kings Cross to Leeds until March 5, 1989, a week before the Class 91s entered service on the diagrams. The then InterCity East Coast franchise holder Great North Eastern Railway bought it to solve a motive power crisis and entered it into service in March 1997, but it suffered a major failure in 2001 and was withdrawn.

After two years of looking after it at Barrow Hill, the AC Locomotive Group bought it for preservation in December 2006. ROBIN JONES

Mallard basks in the sunshine at Barrow Hill Live on September 28, 2013. This scene can never be repeated, for the twin century-old 100ft chimneys of the adjacent brickworks in Campbell Drive, a popular backdrop for enthusiast photographers were blown up on December 12. The brickworks had already been closed by owner the Phoenix Brick Company which had deemed the site to be no longer viable. ROBIN JONES

Mallard was accompanied on its mini tour by one of its successors, Class 55 Deltic No. 55019 *Royal Highland Fusilier*, seen parked in front of the A4 during Barrow Hill Live. ROBIN JONES

Following its autumn tour, *Mallard* is seen being towed through York station by preserved Class 56 No. 56301 en route to its National Railway Museum home, in readiness for the autumn Great Gathering. NRM

The connecting rods being fixed back in position ready for the coming big show. NRM

CHAPTER FIVE

Doncaster Museum remembers the speed kings

Right: The headline from the *Daily Express* of July 4, 1938, says it all. Britain's transport technology was back on top of the world, and the country's public were loving every second.

Coinciding with the National Railway Museum's Mallard 75 celebrations was a landmark exhibition mounted by Doncaster Museum & Art Gallery in honour of the town's greatest 'racehorse'.

Titled *Mallard – a Doncaster Thoroughbred Exhibition*, it showcased many artefacts connected with the A4s, the 1938 speed record run and also their designer.

Rare artefacts from the Doncaster Grammar School railway collection, never before seen in public, were displayed in the free-to-enter museum in Chequer Road.

The school collection includes the original Royal Canadian coat of arms, borrowed by the National Railway Museum to help restorers of *Dominion of Canada* create a facsimile.

Several of the letters written by Sir Nigel Gresley were displayed, with some on letterheaded paper from hotels in Cornwall where he took summer holidays.

Most of them were written to his chief clerk at the LNER, Harry Harper. In one of the letters, written from Paris, Gresley states he has scrapped ideas for glass-topped tables on his trains, and will be placing small pads on them to prevent glasses and bottles from sliding.

One of the cabinets contained his notebook from 1898, with basic sketches of locomotives, four decades before the world speed record achievement.

There were several models ranging from a 5in gauge A4 *Golden Eagle* built by apprentices at 'The Plant' to a 'Minor Great Gathering' of several O gauge A4 models, highlighting different liveries carried by the class.

Terence Cuneo's original masterpiece *Giants Refreshed* which was used for the famous LNER poster

of the same name was also on show.

The biggest exhibit of all was Sir Nigel's boardroom table, on which the original designs for his LNER Pacifics would have been displayed at Doncaster.

Museum manager Carolyn Dalton said: "They say genius is 1% inspiration, 99% perspiration, and Sir Nigel Gresley was definitely one of the hardest workers."

The exhibition, which opened on September 6, 2013, at the start of the St Leger Festival Week, proved so popular that it was extended until February 9, 2014, the weekend when the Festival of British Railway Modelling was held at Doncaster Racecourse, and the weekend before the start of the Great Goodbye. ■

A magnificent gauge 1 model of No. 2509 *Silver Link*, described by the museum as "the ultimate art deco style icon". On September 27, 1935, it made its press debut on the 'Silver Jubilee' train, paving the way for another 34 A4s to follow. ROBIN JONES

"A Knight of the Iron Road"
SIR NIGEL GRESLEY, C.B.E.
President
INSTITUTION OF MECHANICAL ENGINEERS
1936-37

A caricature of Gresley highlighting his election as president of the Institute of Mechanical Engineers.

GIANTS REFRESHED

"PACIFICS" IN THE L·N·E·R LOCOMOTIVE WORKS, DONCASTER

PUBLISHED BY THE LONDON & NORTH EASTERN RAILWAY (A-P 1175)   PRINTED IN GREAT BRITAIN   WATERLOW & SONS LIMITED, LONDON & DUNSTABLE.

Giants Refreshed: the poster by the late Terence Cuneo (1907-1996) subtitled Pacifics in the LNER Locomotive Works, Doncaster. It depicts the inside of the Crimpsall paint shop with workers adding the final touches to the reconditioning of two locomotives. The A4 is No. 1 (60001), original named *Garganey* when outshopped on April 26, 1938, but renamed *Sir Ronald Matthews* from March 1939, It was withdrawn on October 12, 1964. The LNER A2/3 Pacific to the left is No. 520 *Owen Tudor*. Cuneo was commissioned to produce the painting as a publicity poster for LNER. It was the first of a series of posters for the 'Big Four' leading to Cuneo being regarded one of the most important artists of the age of steam. British Railways also used it as a poster. NRM

The 'minor Great Gathering' of seven O gauge A4s at Doncaster Museum: No. 2512 *Silver Fox* in silver livery, No. 4495 *Golden Fleece*, which hauled the 'West Riding Limited' and was originally painted in Great Northern Railway green, also known as 'Doncaster green';
No. 4491 *Commonwealth of Australia*, in garter blue livery honouring the Order of the Garter, No. 4498 *Sir Nigel Gresley*, No. 60027 *Merlin* in experimental BR ultramarine livery, No. 60008 *Dwight D. Eisenhower* and No. 60022 *Mallard* both in British Railways' green livery.

The chime whistle from A4 No. 4491 *Commonwealth of Australia* is now part of the Doncaster Grammar School collection.
ROBIN JONES

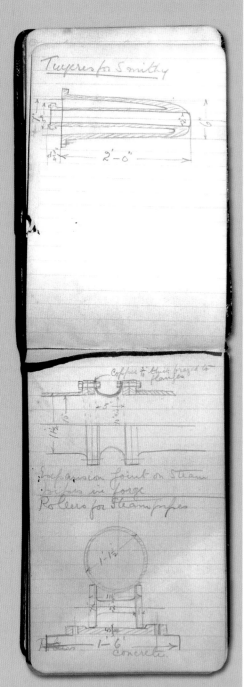

Above: Gresley's notebook of 1898 containing technical drawings. The year before, Gresley completed his formal apprenticeship for the London & North Western Railway at Crewe under Francis Webb. He moved to the Lancashire & Yorkshire Railway's drawing office in 1898. The notebook is part of the Doncaster Grammar School railway collection.

The worksplate from A4 No. 2510 (60015) *Quicksilver*, which was outshopped on September 21, 1935, and withdrawn on April 25, 1963.

Right: Doncaster Racecourse hosted Britain's first aviation meeting from October 18-23 1909, and the Great Northern Railway was quick to cash in. There were trophies and cash prizes for the various events. American, and self-styled 'Colonel' Samuel Franklin Cody even changed his nationality in order to compete for the *Daily Mail* prize of £1000 for flying a mile-long circular route by an all-British aircraft and pilot. Cody failed in his attempt and the prize was taken by JTC Moore-Brabazon a few days later.

Above: Gresley's favourite destination for summer holidays appears to have been Great Western Railway territory. On display at the museum exhibition were letterheaded letters from the Carlyon Bay Hotel near St Austell in Cornwall, and also from the Tregenna Castle Hotel near St Ives, which shares the name of GWR record-breaking 4-6-0 No. 5006 *Tregenna Castle*. On June 6, 1932, it hauled the six-coach 'Cheltenham Flyer' over the 77.3 miles from Swindon to Paddington in 56 minutes 47 seconds, achieving an average speed of 81mph. No other steam train has ever run from start to stop at more than 80mph.

Above: This boardroom table and set of Queen Anne revival style chairs was made in the pattern shop at Doncaster Works around 1905. The table was made using heavy frames and cross-bracing, just as wooden coaches or wagons would be constructed. One of the chairs, a carver, would been used by Gresley when visiting the works, and later by his successors Edward Thompson and Arthur Peppercorn. In the late 1960s, the set was taken to London and used as boardroom furniture for the British Railways' board at Euston House. It was presented to Doncaster Museum & Art Gallery by the Railway Heritage Trust in the mid-Nineties.
ROBIN JONES

The nameplate from A4 No. 4902 (60033) *Seagull*, which was outshopped on June 28, 1935, and withdrawn on December 29, 1963.

The nameplate from the third A4, No. 2511 (60016) *Silver King*, which was outshopped on November 5, 1935, and withdrawn on March 19, 1965.

This superb scale model of A4 No. 4482 *Golden Eagle* was made by apprentices at Doncaster Works.

Left: The original Canadian crest from No. 4489 *Dominion of Canada*, now owned by Doncaster Grammar School. It was temporarily borrowed to create a replica during the restoration of the locomotive at the Locomotion museum in Shildon during 2013.

Below: The register of staff at the LNER, showing the entry for Gresley's principal assistant, Oliver Bulleid.

Above: Gresley's own copy of the Great Northern Railway's Rules & Regulations of 1916, part of the Doncaster Grammar School collection.

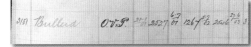

A predecessor to the A4s: LNER experimental W1 No. 10000 (also known as Hush-Hush due to its initial secrecy) was fitted with a high-pressure water-tube boiler, was based on a Gresley 4-6-2 chassis, but with an additional axle to accommodate the extra length. It was the only standard gauge 4-6-4 tender engine to run on a British railway. Built at Darlington Works in 1929, and running non-stop London-Edinburgh services to time in 1930, it suffered from poor steaming and was rebuilt at Doncaster with a modified A4 boiler in 1936, together with three simple expansion cylinders on the normal Gresley layout. Renumbered 60700 under British Railways, it was withdrawn on June 1, 1959 and scrapped at Doncaster. One of the numberplates is seen alongside an O gauge model.

CHAPTER SIX

The Autumn
Great Gathering

This picture was taken at 10am when the museum opened at the start of the Autumn Great Gathering on October 26. Within 10 minutes, the Great Hall was packed with visitors, and it remained that way for the rest of the day. ROBIN JONES

H ow do you follow one of the most successful museum events ever held in Britain, just three months later?

The first Great Gathering in July 2013 attracted a total attendance of 138,141, making it the most successful in the history of the National Railway Museum.

Yet would the public appetite be strong enough to justify a second line-up event at the museum in the autumn? The answer was a resounding yes.

The Autumn Great Gathering, which began on Saturday, October 26, and incorporated the school half-term week, was extended to 17 days, due to the owners of the operational three

A4s not recalling their engines for a further three days than was previously anticipated.

Admission was again free, with visitors being invited to each make a donation at the entrance, while extra charges were made for ticketed events such as early bird photographic sessions, where enthusiasts were able to take pictures of the magnificent six minus the crowds that impaired their vision during normal opening times.

Four of the six survivors were shunted into place in the Great Hall of the National Railway Museum in York on Tuesday, October 15.

No. 4464 *Bittern*, No. 4468 *Mallard* and temporarily repatriated pair No. 4489

Dominion of Canada and No. 60008 *Dwight D. Eisenhower* were later joined by No. 60007 *Sir Nigel Gresley* and No. 60009 *Union of South Africa*.

By the end of the first day of the autumn event, nearly 12,000 people had turned up to see the line-up, followed by another 8000 on the Sunday.

However, even with the extra days, the attendance did not surpass the number of visitors to the summer event. Yet the total attendance of 108,419 was still hailed as an incredible achievement and a resounding testimony to the enduring appeal of Gresley's streamlined masterpieces.

A MYSTERY SOLVED

During the Autumn Great Gathering, museum researchers solved the mystery of the hitherto unnamed guard who appeared in a photograph of the *Mallard* train crew after the record run.

LNER goods guard Henry 'Harry' Croucher was pictured alongside the rest of the train crew in several seminal photographs taken after the run on July 3, 1938.

However, his identity remained a mystery until his daughter Julie Slater from London contacted the museum's associate curator of railway vehicles Bob Gwynne and arranged to visit the event on November 8 with her son Richard Slater from Nottingham.

Julie produced family photographs to prove that her dad was on board the train as it raced down Stoke Bank after being drafted in as part of the world steam speed record attempt team, unsuspecting, as were the rest of the crew, of what the true purpose of the 'braking test' trip was.

Her late brother Bert also worked for the LNER before he died in a naval battle while serving during the Second World War.

Bob said: "Our Mallard 75 celebrations have given us a new strand in the *Mallard* story. There is absolutely no doubt that the man in the family photos Julie provided is the same man as in the picture taken of the record-breaking crew at Peterborough.

"Harry would have been quite pleased at being asked to work on that Sunday's 'brake trial' as it would have meant double time, but of all the crew in the picture he looks like he found it quite a hair-raising experience.

"Unfortunately he had already died before our 50th anniversary celebrations, so it has taken the added publicity surrounding the 75th anniversary to encourage Julie and her family to step forward and talk about their strong connection to our celebrity locomotive."

In the Great Hall, Julie said: "I feel overwhelmed that I'm here. Now I can let everyone know who my father was."

IN THE BLACK

Before the Great Gatherings were staged, there had been criticism of the cost of temporarily repatriating *Dwight D. Eisenhower* and *Dominion of Canada* for the event.

The repatriation was heavily sponsored, but the museum later disclosed that the cost would be $231,000.

Left: The three LNER garter blue A4s – *Bittern, Mallard* and *Dominion of Canada* – again lined up together. NRM

Below: Stairs were provided so that visitors could see inside the cabs of the A4s, prompting long queues through the days of the Great Gatherings. The cab of No. 60008 *Dwight D. Eisenhower* was cosmetically refurbished along with the exterior of the locomotive. ROBIN JONES

Seats were at a premium in the Mallard cafe inside the Great Hall throughout the line-ups.

Should we be spending that sort of taxpayers' money in a recession, and depleting the reserves of the Science Museum Group, the question was asked.

However, those who visited one or both events had another question to ask. After standing for hours in queues at the museum's three catering outlets to get served and seeing mountains of souvenirs in the retail outlets quickly denuded, everyone began asking – how much money are they making?

Confounding the initial critics, once the museum had done its sums, it was found that even before the Great Goodbye was held at the Locomotion museum in Shildon, a total of £404,500 'profit' to be reinvested in the Science Museum group had been made.

The figures were broken down as follows:

Firstly, the NRM received cash sponsorship and donations towards the Mallard 75 celebrations of £242,271 which more than covered the specific costs of bringing *Dominion of Canada* and *Dwight D. Eisenhower* home and safely returning them at the end of the two-year loan period.

LNER goods guard Harry Croucher is fourth on the right in the now legendary picture of *Mallard's* crew after the record breaking run taken at Peterborough. Also pictured are fireman Thomas Bray, driver Joe Duddington and inspector Sam Jenkins. NRM

The transcontinental move, as outlined in our Mallard 75 volume, was brought within the Science Museum's financial grasp only thanks to the received £260,000 and promised £240,000 of in-kind support from the museum's project partners including haulage company Moveright International, shipping company ACL, Peel Ports in the UK plus Ceres and Canadian National Railways in Canada.

The Science Museum Group provided just over £231,000 capital support to the overall Mallard 75 project which in addition to the

repatriation costs, an identical figure, also included all aspects of the display of the 'big six'. That ranged from the ceremonial shunt of *Mallard* on July 3 in front of the world media to more mundane expenses such as specially designed stairs for footplate access – a big winner with the public at both York events – essential asbestos remediation work and insurance.

The £231,000 repatriation and return figure is a projected cost based on actual and estimated expenditure by the museum and its

Julie Slater, granddaughter of world speed record 'mystery' guard Harry Croucher, in the cab of *Mallard* during the Autumn Great Gathering. NRM

The replica of *Dominion of Canada's* coat of arms as meticulously recreated by Bury-based Heritage Painting. ROBIN JONES

project partners, and not only covers insurance, asbestos remediation, hire costs and rail movements, but also includes a sizeable contingency fund for any problems arising in regard to the return journey.

However, as the mechanics of the transatlantic were plotted in detail by haulier Andrew Goodman on the outward journey, it was hoped that this contingency will not be necessary.

Although a drop in the ocean in museum redevelopment terms – by comparison, the British Museum's extension to house its new world conservation and exhibitions centre has cost £135 million – the figure nonetheless comprised a sizeable investment in today's cash-strapped environment.

The commercial turnover for the first two Great Gatherings was over £1 million, providing a return to the Science Museum Group of nearly £497,000 – a tremendous return on investment for a not-for-profit organisation whose measure for success is the volume of people it educates and informs about science and engineering.

During the events, visitors gave a total of just under £140,000 in donations at the door, plus gift aid.

The museum brought in a further £50,000 with its ticketed photography and dining events.

During the first Great Gathering, the Friends of the National Railway Museum took £76,000, the profit from which should have more than covered the group's donation of £50,000 towards the cosmetic restoration of the two North American A4s.

Furthermore, *Mallard*'s September appearances at Grantham, Doncaster and Barrow Hill earned £6000 in loan fees.

The commercial statistics were more than impressive. In early 2014, the total cash sponsorship and donations for the Mallard 75 project were said to be £242,300. While the total forecast cost was given as £530,700, once income from nearly a quarter of a million visitors had been taken into account, £404,500 was left over to be invested in the work of the Science Museum Group.

A museum spokesman said: "The National Railway Museum, like all national museums, is a not-for-profit organisation and its specific mission is to enable people to have a life-enhancing experience through exploring the story of railways. 'Big wow' events like the Great Gatherings are perhaps one of the few ways museums can attract repeat visits and pull in new visitors in these times of austerity when a day out for the family has to be carefully considered.

Crowds clamoured to inspect and photograph the six A4s throughout the 17-day event.
ROBIN JONES

Below: During the Autumn Great Gathering, the museum's souvenir shop did a brisk trade in these attractive large ceramic Mallard tiles, priced £25 each. ROBIN JONES

Above: The repatriated A4s, *Dwight D. Eisenhower* (left) and *Dominion of Canada*, which many people thought would never be seen in Britain again, with *Mallard* in-between. ROBIN JONES

Right: The bell presented to No. 4489 on March 17, 1938, back in place following its reversion to its as-built form. ROBIN JONES

"Ask any one of those visitors in July and October if they found it a life-enhancing experience and I am sure they will answer in the affirmative. Although it was a major undertaking to bring two Doncaster-built locomotives home to the UK for a two-year visit, the resulting news splash got people talking about *Mallard* and the anniversary.

"The bold scheme to bring together all six surviving members of the A4 class and the engineering ingenuity required to extract the borrowed locos and transport them home also fitted perfectly with the overall mission of the Science Museum Group, which is to engage people in a dialogue about the history, present and future of human ingenuity in the fields of science, technology, medicine, transport and media.

"The Great Gathering events also fitted in with the essence of the NRM which is to connect generations through the wonderful stories of railways and how they shape our world."

No. 60008 *Dwight D. Eisenhower* in one of the quieter moments. ROBIN JONES

Above and below: These classic LNER A4 posters were included in the museum's It's Quicker by Rail exhibition which ran from July 4 until November to coincide with the two Great Gatherings. NRM

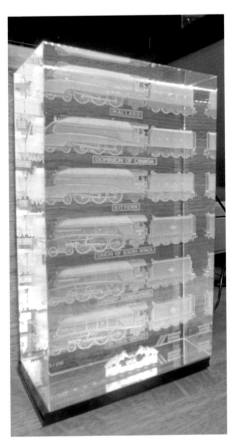

Above: A premier product produced on behalf of the museum to mark Mallard 75 is this sizeable illuminated paperweight containing images of all six surviving A4s, priced at £225.

Right: Souvenir mug produced for Mallard 75. NRM

Figures showed that museum visitor numbers by January 2014 had soared by 35% on the previous year – and, accordingly, 900,000 visitors for the financial year 2013/14 were forecasted, against the original estimate of 700,000.

At its autumn annual conference, local tourism organisation Visit York praised Mallard 75 for the best visitor numbers to the city in decades.

CHAPTER SEVEN

The last run of driver Joe Burgess (right) on April 27, 1953. Fireman Alfred Smith is in the background. The pair worked on *Mallard* for four years in the Forties. At the autumn Great Gathering, Alf described Joe as an "engineman, not a driver, a real gentleman" and the A4s as "engines built miles before their time." He said that 100mph was no problem for A4s, and he had records of them reaching 115mph. NRM

They made it happen!

There is no doubting the magnificence of the LNER A4 streamlined Pacifics and the brilliance of their design.

However, the performance of any locomotive can only be only as good as the men on the footplate.

When Steve Davies dreamed up plans to repatriate No. 60008 *Dwight D. Eisenhower* and No. 60010 *Dominion of Canada* for a unique line-up of all six survivors, it was his associate curator of rail vehicles, Bob Gwynne, who suggested staging the biggest reunion of A4 fireman and drivers held in the heritage era.

For two years, as arrangements were made to bring the two Pacifics back across the Atlantic, and once they were safely here, cosmetic restoration got underway. No stone was left unturned in attempts by NRM researchers to track down the surviving locomen, many now in their eighties and nineties.

More than 90 were contacted, and on October 26, 2013, the first day of the autumn Great Gathering, around 80 footplate veterans were assembled at the museum, many meeting for the first time since the end of steam, exchanging old drivers' tales and reminiscences.

Several of them brought diaries of their days on the footplate and shovel, proudly kept since.

Indeed, so many former drivers and firemen turned up for the event that they had to be divided into two rooms, one for those from King's Cross 'Top Shed' and another for those who were based at other major East Coast Main Line sheds, including Edinburgh Haymarket, York, Doncaster, Gateshead, Peterborough, Carlisle, and

Alfred Smith, a former King's Cross driver, now 92. Walter 'Wally' Blazey is on the far left. NRM

Tony Blaxill, a fireman with experience of A4s running above 100mph. ROBIN JONES

The A4 drivers and firemen from King's Cross 'Top Shed' came together on the first day of the autumn Great Gathering. NRM

Newton Heath. Walter Blazey, 88, a regular fireman on *Dwight D. Eisenhower* for two years, began work as a cleaner at 'Top Shed' in 1941.

His first job was to clean another Gresley masterpiece – the experimental W1 No. 10000 'Hush-Hush', the only 4-6-4 tender locomotive to run in Britain. It had hit a bullock the day before, and the remains had to be cleaned off.

He then spent 13 years as a fireman on A4s, before he working as a driver for 25 years. In total, he spent 48 years' service at the legendary King's Cross shed.

Walter also fired on No. 60003 *Andrew K. McCosh* when it was being fitted with AWS equipment, and recalls the corridor in the tender being filled up with batteries; he also spent four months on No. 60006 *Sir Ralph Wedgwood.*

Walter broke his arm when he was a fireman on an A4 by catching it on the water scoop handle on the tender as he took on water at speed at Balby, south of Doncaster.

In the 1950s, he recalled taking *Bittern* past Essendine – a stone's throw from Little Bytham, scene of *Mallard*'s world speed record, at 117mph.

Like many of his fellow East Coast Main Line drivers of the day, when dieselisation came, Walter went on to drive Class 55 Deltic diesels.

He fondly recalled an occasion where, on a King's Cross to Doncaster turn in 1959, he brought the Royal Train down to 18mph at Potters Bar so sharply that everyone in the sleeping cars including the Duke of Edinburgh fell out of bed.

> **"I USED TO WISH I HAD THE CHANCE TO HAVE ANOTHER GO AT *MALLARD'S* WORLD RECORD BECAUSE I THINK WE COULD HAVE BEATEN IT."**

"Prince Philip walked straight past me," he recalled. Sam Jenkins, the traction inspector – the same who had been on the footplate of *Mallard* as it reached 126mph on July 3, 1938, told him sharply to report to his office the next morning.

After entering with some trepidation, Walter was told that the sudden braking was not his fault, and instead had been traced back to a valve that had not worked correctly.

Alfred Smith, 92, recalled *Mallard* ascending Stoke Bank at 90mph during speed trials in 1952, with King's Cross shedmaster Peter Townend on board.

Suddenly, the connecting road snapped, "and Peter Townend was out of the corridor tender as fast as anyone could move," he recalled.

Tony Blaxill was a fireman on No. 60007 *Sir Nigel Gresley*, alongside driver McKinley (known as 'everything happens to me Mac') on July 21, 1959, when it ascended the gradient to Stoke Tunnel at 90mph. It was only two months before that the same locomotive had set a postwar steam record speed of 112mph locally.

Grantham was passed above the permitted 70mph, and soon No. 60007 was running at a constant 100mph, the flat crossing at Newark-on-Trent again being passed in excess of the speed limit.

On May 23, 1952, he was interviewed by Wynford Vaughan-Thomas on a BBC schools programme on the theme of I Want to Be An Engine Driver. Baxill explained all the intricacies of operating *Mallard* to him on camera.

Maurice Dakin worked on all six surviving A4s under British Railways. ROBIN JONES

A4 locoman Reg Turner, who was based at York. ROBIN JONES

Former drivers and firemen from York shed at the NRM on October 26, 2013. NRM

Former A4 firemen George Purnell once fired for Mallard record-breaking fireman Tommy Bray, who by then had passed out as a driver. NRM

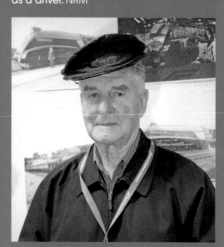
Albert 'Sid' Strachan', who wanted to but did not have a crack at breaking Mallard's official record, but claimed he had driven an A4 well above that speed. NRM

Special pride of place went to Maurice Dakin, who worked on all six surviving A4s during their British Railways' days. "I fired most of the A4s that were at King's Cross," he said. "I enjoyed it all so much – they were all good memories.

Maurice had also attended the first Great Gathering on July 3, 2013, said, "it is fantastic that all six have come together again."

Reg Turner, 91, began as a cleaner in April 1941, was a fireman on the A4s during the Second World War, became passed as a driver in 1961 and ended his railway career driving Class 125 High Speed Trains up to 1987. "The "A4s were very good locomotive," he said. They could hold a speed of 80-85mph quite easily."

He drove A4s until they were withdrawn in the 1960s, including Bittern on one of its last trips.

King's Cross driver Rob Birch, who started on the railways in 1947 at the age of 14, recalled an incident when he was on the footplate of Mallard with the 9.20am from King's Cross when, after passing the water troughs at Newark, a lump of coal flew through a window of a house near a level crossing. Police were called over fears that someone could have been injured.

Former Doncaster locoman George Purnell, who also attended the reunion, had worked as a fireman to driver Tommy Bray, the fireman on Mallard's record-breaking run. He described travelling at speed on an A4 as 'exhilarating.'

George said that he left the railway in 1954 after realising he would never become a driver before steam was phased out… and had no intention of driving diesels.

Anthony Coulls, the NRM's senior curator of rail vehicles, spoke to Albert 'Sid' Strachan, who was based at Doncaster and now lives at Balby. Sid said that he had known Joe Duddington, the driver on Mallard's record run

Former A4 locomotive crews reminisce about the good old days. ROBIN JONES

Gateshead shed veteran Beresford Bowes talking to Bob Gwynne. NRM

John Black and Hugh Jones, who worked at Doncaster Works. NRM

"YOU DIDN'T GET THE CHANCE TO PUT YOUR SHOVEL DOWN. I WOULD BE SHIFTING SIX TO EIGHT TONNES OF COAL ON EACH TRIP, BUT I GOT USED TO IT."

John Anthony and his wife at the reception for A4 locomen on October 26. NRM

A4 veteran Harry Wilson in front of a montage of the museum's A4 photographs. The drivers who attended the reunion added names to many other staff in the pictures which the museum had hitherto been unable to identify. NRM

– and claimed that he himself had been on the footplate of an A4 that had run significantly faster than No. 4468 achieved on that day, well above 130mph. However, Anthony said afterwards that there have been several similar claims about A4s unofficially exceeding 126mph, but no corroborative evidence existed.

Aged 18, Sid had begun work at the Doncaster Carr yard after transferring from 'The Plant'. He said, "I asked if I could be a fireman at 18 and by the time I was 26 I was a driver, just working in the depot. You had to be experienced before you could drive on the main line so I spent time as a fireman.

"You didn't get the chance to put your shovel down. I would be shifting six to eight tonnes of coal on each trip, but I got used to it.

"I used to wish I had the chance to have another go at *Mallard*'s world record because I think we could have beaten it."

Many of the locomen spoke of an age in which the driver's word was law.

One driver at King's Cross was so protective of his personal space on the footplate that he drew a demarcation line in chalk and told his fireman never to step over it.

The long, arduous, backbreaking hours of driving a steam locomotive along the ECML ended with dieselisation, which at a stroke brought vastly improved working conditions.

However, when asked at the end of a question-and-answer session whether they would do it all over again in the steam era, the five-man panel of drivers were unanimous. Most certainly, they said.

Bob Gwynne said: "This must be one of the biggest get-togethers of steam loco crews in recent times.

"Given that many of the people who got in touch as a result of July's Mallard 75 celebrations are well beyond retirement age we were amazed that so many could join us to form a special Great Gathering of former A4 crews.

"Our event is not only an opportunity for them to see the 'Big Six' on the first day of our autumn Great Gathering, but a long-awaited chance to meet up with former colleagues and share colourful experiences of working as scheduled crew on the East Coast Main Line, surrounded by archive photos to get their memories flowing." ∎

Retired locoman Preston Kyme reunited with an A4 at the autumn Great Gathering. NRM

CHAPTER EIGHT

New light
on the
steam era's

The six A4s as they have never been seen before and never will be again: 21st century theatrical lighting technology illuminates Gresley's masterpieces in the Locos In A Different Light competition inside the Great Hall. KIPPA MATTHEWS/NRM

N° 4489
CLASS
A4

THE GREAT GATHERING

finest

The Mallard 75 logo projected on to the wall of the Great Hall during the Locos In A Different Light contest. ROBIN JONES

Just like old days: the firebox in *Union of South Africa* glows again, illuminating the cab interior. ROBIN JONES

During the Autumn Great Gathering, the six A4s were showcased in a way that even Sir Nigel Gresley would never have envisaged.

The hugely-successful event at the NRM encompassed the fifth annual Locos In a Different Light competition.

This contest, staged as part of the wider Illuminating York festival, saw the line-up of six A4s bathed in theatrical lighting and artificial smoke effects by teams of students from all over Britain.

Theatricality, energy consumption, conservation and safety, not necessarily the most striking exhibit, were the criteria by which the teams were judged by industry professionals at a VIP preview evening on October 29.

The newly-opened Da Vinci Studio School of Creative Enterprise in Letchworth, Hertfordshire, whose students illuminated *Dominion of Canada* in fluorescent lighting which reflected that nation's flag, was the winner.

The school's creative lighting effects brought *Mallard*'s freshly cosmetically-restored sister engine *Dominion of Canada* to life, with subtle steam effects, a highlighted headboard and bell and dramatic red side lighting to provide contrast for its gleaming garter blue paint.

Its students' work scored particularly highly on safety and conservation as the lights were not mounted on the locomotive itself.

Mark Waites from the Da Vinci Studio School said: "The lads are overjoyed with their win; it's a fantastic achievement for us as we only opened at the beginning of last month (September 2013). To say we are chuffed is an understatement."

Coming second was York College, whose students lit up *Union of South Africa*, and in third place was the University of South Wales, which tackled *Mallard*.

The 2012 winners, Kent-based Rose Bruford College, whose students were assigned to *Sir Nigel Gresley*, finished fourth, followed by Barking & Dagenham College with *Bittern* and University of South Wales with *Dwight D. Eisenhower*.

The winning Da Vinci School team and *Dominion of Canada*. **KIPPA** MATTHEWS/NRM

BR Brunswick green-liveried No. 60009 *Union of South Africa* becomes bathed in a golden aura. DAN CLARKSON/NRM

Above: *Dwight D. Eisenhower* and *Union of South Africa* together during Locos In A Different Light. JAMES SHUTTLEWORTH

Left and Below: Once more, a glow is emitted from the cab of *Union of South Africa* inside what was once York North locomotive shed. ROBIN JONES

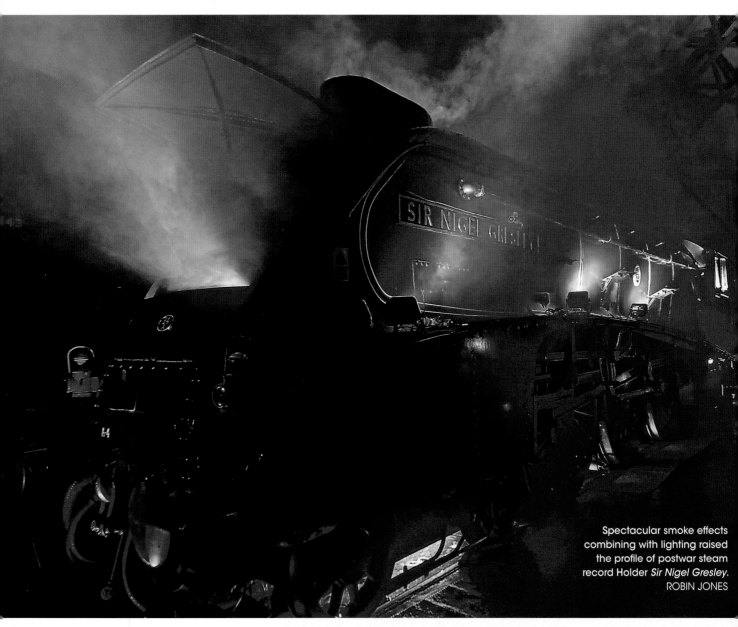

Spectacular smoke effects combining with lighting raised the profile of postwar steam record Holder *Sir Nigel Gresley*. ROBIN JONES

Mallard 75 project manager Tobias Lumb, who was one of the judges, said: "Our annual lighting competition has always been a huge success, and this Locos in a Different Light has been our greatest yet. The calibre of the students work has been impressive and the judges had a tough task in picking a winner."

During the following four evenings, the event, sponsored by AC Special Projects, was open to the public free of charge.

Over and above the bumper daytime attendances, Locos In a Different Light attracted 10,399 visitors – a figure which compares very favourably with a well-attended gala at a top heritage railway over the same period.

The Illuminating York Festival also featured artworks projected on the city's Clifford's Tower and the Yorkshire Museum, with candlelit tours of Barley Hall, the Mansion House, the Merchant Taylors' Hall, Fairfax House and the Merchant Adventurers' Hall. The festival was supported by City of York Council, Arts Council England, Visit York, York St John University, English Heritage, York Museums Trust and York Archaeological Trust.

Above: Lighting being installed at the start of the contest. KIPPA MATTHEWS/NRM

Left: *Mallard*, illuminated by students from the University of South Wales, came third in the judging. ROBIN JONES

Above: Hey – I'm not an A4, but can I join in too? While students were busy lighting up the A4s, their lecturers tackled other exhibits inside the Great Hall, including LMS Stanier 2-6-4T No. 2500, which took on something of a German steam locomotive appearance. ROBIN JONES

Left and far left: *Bittern*, the heritage era steam speed record holder following its 92.5mph run in July 2013. ROBIN JONES

CHAPTER NINE

Sons of *Mallard!*

GRESLEY'S LNER A4s are by no means the only type of streamlined Pacific to grace these shores. The Southern Railway also had its own fleet, in three different variations – the Merchant Navy 4-6-2s and their lighter counterparts the West Country and Battle of Britain classes. Examples of all three classes can be seen in action in Britain today, not only on the main line but on heritage railways too.

There are many differences between the LNER and SR streamliners, but one crucial link. The man who was Gresley's assistant when he designed the A4s, and who has been credited with influencing their distinctive shape, was the man who devised their Southern counterparts, Oliver Vaughan Snell

Bulleid. The son of British immigrants William Bulleid, a Devon farmer from North Tawton, and Marian Pugh, he was born on September 19, 1882, in Invercargill, New Zealand.

After William died from pleurisy, the family went to live in his mother's home town of Llanfyllin in Powys.

From the age of 11 to 13, young Oliver attended Spa College at the Bridge of Allan, Stirlingshire, and then Accrington Technical College. In his spare time, he used the tools and lathe in his uncle's workshop.

Oliver's cousin, the Reverend Edgar Lee, was friendly with Great Northern Railway locomotive superintendent Henry Alfred Ivatt. Rebutting his family's wishes for him to pursue a law career in New Zealand, Oliver became a

Doncaster Works apprentice on January 21, 1901.

Four years later, he became personal assistant to the works manager, but in 1908 took a new job with the French division of Westinghouse Electric Corporation – Société Anonyme Westinghouse – in Paris. That year, he also married Ivatt's youngster daughter Marjorie, thanks to his much bigger salary. While abroad, Bulleid also acted as a mechanical engineer for the Board of Trade at continental exhibitions.

However, despite his departure, he had left a very favourable impression during his formative years with the GNR, for in 1912 the company made him an offer he could not refuse.

MALLARD DNA IN THEIR DESIGNS? Rebuilt Merchant Navy Pacific No. 35005 *Canadian Pacific*, unrebuilt Battle of Britain 4-6-2 No. 34070 *Manston* and West Country No. 34028 *Eddystone* at the Eastleigh 100 event, marking the centenary of the LSWR's Eastleigh Works, and which attracted 19,000 visitors over the May 23-25, 2009 spring bank holiday weekend. BRIAN SHARPE

Oliver became chief technical assistant to Gresley, who was only six years older.

When the First World War broke out, Oliver volunteered for service. He was quickly elevated to the rank of major and was appointed deputy assistant director of railway traffic.

The year after the conflict ended, he became manager of the GNR's carriage and wagon works.

After the Grouping of 1923, Gresley took Bulleid back to Doncaster, again as his assistant but this time with a far wider remit. Their job now was to design new powerful locomotives for the LNER.

Bulleid did not work alongside Gresley as he designed the great Pacifics, but had a

significant influence on their design. Indeed, several historians share the credit for the distinctive outline of the A4s between Gresley and Bulleid.

In Mallard 75, we saw how the distinctive air-smoothed shape of the A4s was influenced to some extent by the French Bugatti petrol railcar which appeared in 1933. One of them, No. 24408 *Presidential*, set a new world speed record of 122mph in 1934. The railcars in turn had been influenced by Italian racing car designer and manufacturer Ettore Bugatti's Royale series of cars.

HA Ivatt had been introduced to Bugatti by former Doncaster Works' apprentice Walter Owen Bentley, who had worked with Gresley, and whose surname became a household word

for luxury cars. Gresley and Bulleid often visited Bugatti at his French home, sharing his interest in motor sport. Bugatti had undertaken exhaustive tests with wind tunnels to tackle aerodynamics before producing his most successful racing car of all, the Type 35. Bugatti also took the pair on railcar trips from Paris to Le Havre in 1933.

It was Bulleid who was credited with designing the aerofoil streamlined side skirts or valances fitted to all the A4s as built, but removed during the Second World War to improve access to the valve gear for maintenance and were not replaced afterwards. Unlike their great rivals, the LMS Princess Coronation Pacifics, the A4s kept the rest of their streamlined casings to the end.

Right: Reclaiming lost Southern territory in style: Battle of Britain light Pacific No. 34067 *Tangmere* heads the first steam train from London over the Swanage Branch since the heritage railway which occupied the western end was reconnected to the main line. The train was Past-Time Rail's 'Wessex Venturer', carrying a 'Royal Wessex' headboard, and is seen approaching Cat's Eye bridge and Swanage Railway metals on May 2, 2009. ROBIN JONES

The same can be said of very few other streamlined classes worldwide.

The A4 Pacifics were designed for high-speed passenger services, and the streamlining was there not only to improve aerodynamics, and therefore speed, but also to create an updraught to lift smoke away from the driver's vision as an alternative to the more common smoke deflectors.

Bulleid was also heavily involved with other Gresley big engines, notably the P1 and P2 class 2-8-2s and the one-off articulated U1 Beyer-Garratt No. 2395. In the case of the P2s, all six engines eventually received the distinctive streamlined front end found on the A4.

In 1934, Bulleid went to France with the first P2, No. 2001 *Cock o' the North*, when it was taken there for tests. The following year, he was on the footplate of A1 No. 4472 *Flying Scotsman* when it made a high speed run to Leeds to test the timing of the new 'Silver Jubilee' service, launched that year behind A4 No. 2509 *Silver Link* and comprising the streamlined carriages that he had designed.

Bulleid might have stayed with the LNER, maybe taking over from Gresley and honing the Pacific concept to even greater heights and faster speeds.

However, he would not be at Gresley's side when *Mallard* took the world steam record on July 3, 1938, for by then he had, at the age of 55, been installed as the chief mechanical engineer of the Southern Railway.

He was head-hunted for the job because of the failing health of the SR's chief mechanical engineer Richard Maunsell. Interviewed by SR general manager Sir Herbert Walker on May 11, 1937, Bulleid took over the position on October 1 that year.

The Southern Railway was the most financially successful of the 'Big Four' companies, largely thanks to the vast progresss it made with both suburban and main line third-rail electrification.

However, because of Maunsell's condition, SR locomotive development had been placed on hold after the successful introduction of the Schools class 4-4-0s in 1930, and with regard to steam it was falling behind the other three.

Now the SR had arguably one of the best CMEs in the country, a man with first-hand knowledge of Gresley

Pacifics with their free steaming boilers and fast three-cylinder layout.

In 1938, Bulleid was given the go ahead by Walker's successor as general manager, Gilbert Szlumper, to produce designs for 20 express passenger locomotives.

Bulleid took the same stance as Gresley had done when he designed the A4s. His aim was to produce a superior and modern steam locomotive that would be a genuine alternative to diesel and electric traction, not just stop-gaps until the inevitable and steam was withdrawn en masse.

At first, Bulleid opted for a 4-8-2 which would be capable of hauling the heavy 'Golden Arrow' and 'Night Ferry' continental expresses. The idea was soon changed

West Country light Pacific No. 34006 *Bude* heads out of Bournemouth Central in 1965. ANDREW PM WRIGHT COLLECTION

Battle of Britain Pacific No. 34051 *Winston Churchill* heading the Locomotive Club of Great Britain's 'Wessex Downsman' railtour at Bournemouth West station on April 4, 1965. Originally numbered 21C151, it was officially named *Winston Churchill* in a ceremony at Waterloo on September 11, 1947. The former prime minister, by then Leader of the Opposition, was offered the chance to name the locomotive but turned it down, claiming a prior engagement.

No. 34051 was chosen to head Sir Winston Churchill's funeral train on January 30, 1965, taking his coffin from Waterloo to Handborough, the nearest station to his final resting place, the churchyard at Bladon.

Accordingly, it was earmarked for preservation as part of the National Collection in September 1965. After spending decades as a static exhibit in the National Railway Museum in York, No. 34051 was moved in 2012 to the Mid-Hants Railway's Ropley Works for a

£44,000 cosmetic restoration, the money being raised by the Friends of the National Railway Museum South of England Group.

It is hoped to unveil the locomotive again in time for the 50th anniversary of the funeral in 2015. All six carriages from the funeral train survive, and in the wake of the Mallard 75 successes, the NRM has been looking at reassembling it for another headline-grabbing special event.
ANDREW PM WRIGHT COLLECTION

to a 2-8-2, but both designs met with resistance on some SR quarters.

The compromise was a new Pacific, one that would be equally at home on express and semi-fast services, with Bulleid building on his first-hand expert knowledge of the Gresley types.

The SR's plan for a Pacific fleet of its own was stalled somewhat, but not derailed, by the outbreak of the Second World War, as armaments and munitions production by necessity took priority.

The wartime Coalition government banned the building of express passenger locomotives due to shortages of materials and a need for engines with freight-hauling capabilities. Accordingly, Bulleid's new Pacifics were to have a nominal mixed traffic classification and had to be capable of freight as well as passenger work. It was one way of getting round the ban. Under the direction of Bulleid, the Eastleigh Works drawing office draughtsmen set to work.

Bulleid's first streamlined Merchant Navy Pacific, No. 21C1 *Channel Packet*, emerged from Eastleigh on February 18, 1941, and was officially named at a ceremony at Eastleigh Works on March 10, by the then Minister for Transport Lieutenant-Colonel J T C Moore-Brabazon.

He drove the locomotive along sidings and up to a train, remarking that its designer was "not only an engineer, but an artist". The class members were named after the Merchant Navy shipping lines involved in the Battle of the Atlantic, and latterly those which used Southampton Docks, which the SR opened during this period. A total of 30 would eventually be built.

Its streamlined shape was distinctive as that of the A4s, but its main purpose was not aerodynamics, as evidenced by the extremely flat front end for smoke deflection. In this and several other aspects, Bulleid's Pacifics diverged from Gresley's.

The flat sides were also an aid to cleaning the locomotive with a carriage washer in a bid to reduce labour costs.

Bulleid had long since come to the conclusion that it was far better not to have working parts exposed to the elements where they ended up being plastered by dirt thrown up from the track. He also took the view that steam engines should get nearer to the internal combustion engine, which enclosed the working parts and used pump lubrication to keep it all running smoothly.

The locomotives featured thermic syphons along with Bulleid's revolutionary but controversial chain-driven valve gear. Furthermore, the maximum boiler pressure was higher than any other British regular service locomotive at 280psi.

Electric lighting was also provided on both the

Above: West Country Pacific No. 34007 *Wadebridge* heads past Bewdley South signalbox during a visit to the Severn Valley Railway's March 22-24, 2013 spring steam gala.
DUNCAN LANGTREE

Right: West Country Pacific No. 34046 *Braunton*, one of the more recent additions to the heritage main line fleet, pictured on the turntable at Minehead on the West Somerset Railway, its restoration base.
ROBIN JONES

locomotive and in the cab, supplied by a steam-powered generator fitted below the footplate. The gauges were lit by ultra-violet light, facilitating clearer night-time vision of the boiler steam pressure gauge and the brake pipe vacuum pressure gauge while eliminating dazzle, making it easier for the crew to see signals along the track.

The first two Merchant Navies were considered overweight and accordingly were modified. Indeed, the heavy weight of the Merchant Navies restricted their route availability.

The last of a further batch of eight was delivered in July 1942. The final batch of 10 arrived between December 1944 and June 1945. Ten more Merchant Navies ordered in 1947 were delivered after the formation of British Railways on January 1, 1948.

Continental influence came to the fore when Bulleid introduced a new numbering scheme to the SR. Letters and numbers were used to designate the powered and unpowered axles, and so a Pacific – a 4-6-2 – became 21C1, with C referring to the three driving axles, 2 to the number of powered axles and 1 to the unpowered axles.

To countermand the weight problem with the Merchant Navies, Bulleid came up with a lighter version. No. 21C101 *Exeter*, the first of the Battle of Britain class and West Country class light Pacifics, made its debut in 1945, and eventually a total of 110 of both classes were built.

While the streamlined casings of the A4s earned them the nicknames of 'Streaks', Bulleid's Pacifics became known as 'spam cans'. A distinctive feature of Bulleid's steam locomotives were the wheels. They were of the 'boxpok' type, whereby each wheel is made of box sections rather than having spokes, as in the traditional manner. A major advantage here was the reduction in tyre wear. Bulleid and Firth Brown Steels designed a variation of the original Boxpok wheels that had been patented by a company in Illinois.

Just as several of the A4s were named after birds, an interest of Gresley, so Bulleid's West Country roots were reflected in the names chosen for one of his class of light Pacifics – *Barnstaple, Ottery St Mary, Padstow, Bude, Bideford, Wells, Trevone*…

The Battle of Britain Pacifics were given names after places and heroes connected with the UK's darkest hour and, in the circumstances, greatest triumph.

Bulleid Pacifics were the flagship form of traction in the south and south west of England until the end of steam on the Southern Region in 1967, hauling famous named trains such as the 'Atlantic Coast Express'.

Indeed, the final British Railways steam train into Waterloo was the Weymouth boat express. It was hauled by Merchant Navy No. 35030 *Elder Dempster Lines* on July 9, 1967.

Battle of Britain Pacific No. 34092 *City of Wells* passes Barford St Martin with a Salisbury to Yeovil Junction charter on July 24, 1988. BRIAN SHARPE

Leader at Oxted on November 22, 1949, in an official British Railways photograph.

Bulleid Battle of Britain light Pacific No. 34110 *66 Squadron* was the last to be built, in January 1951. It is seen at Salisbury with the 10am Plymouth (Friary) to Portsmouth & Southsea service on July 23, 1963. BEN BROOKSBANK*

Battle of Britain Pacific No. 34067 *Tangmere* made steam history on May 15, 2011, when it headed the 'Golden Arrow' from St Pancras International to Canterbury. It was the first steam working out of the new International terminus next door to King's Cross, and comprised a private charter to mark the reopening of the Midland Railway's St Pancras Hotel following a multi-million-pound refurbishment. MIKE HOWKINS

In 1959, due to problems with several features of Bulleid's design, all members of the class were rebuilt, all of the Merchant Navies were rebuilt minus their air smoothed casings. Sixty of the light Pacifics were similarly rebuilt between 1957-61.

Bulleid's remit at the Southern was far wider than at the LNER. His first task was to build three six-wheel diesel shunters, and he worked on the designs of main line diesel types including the prototypes Nos. 10201-3. He also designed electric multiple units for the expanding third-rail network, which he did much to improve, and he also experimented with continental-style double-deck coaches.

His last Southern Railway steam locomotive design, however, was far more radical than even Gresley's A4s had been in their day.

Bulleid's Leader class was intended to be five experimental 0-6-6-0T articulated locomotives, diesel-like in appearance, with a cab at either end providing

maximum visibility, and a fireman stoking the firebox in a centre cab.

Just as Gresley and the LNER were determined to show that steam could still do a better job than innovations like the German 'Flying Hamburger', so for Bulleid, Leader was a last throw of the dice for steam.

The prototype Leader, No. 36001, was built at Brighton Works between July 1947 and June 1949. It was the only one to be finished.

After nationalisation, Bulleid continued as chief mechanical engineer of the Southern Region.

However, British Railways ditched the Leader project in 1951 after the prototype failed to impress in trials and crew complained about the scorching hot centre cab and the one at the smokebox end.

By then, Bulleid was away to pastures new, having been appointed as chief mechanical engineer of the Irish railway network Córas Iompair Éireann in 1950

He implemented mass dieselisation. Seven years later,

he produced a peat-burning version of Leader, but it too was a failure.

Bulleid retired in 1958 and moved to mid-Devon. Presented with an honorary doctorate of science by Bath University in 1967, three years later he died in Malta at the age of 87.

A total of 11 Merchant Navies – more than a third of the class – were sold into preservation; similarly 19 light Pacifics have also survived.

The number of 30 seems top heavy when compared to that of the six A4s, only one A2 and A3 and, until a new one was built, no A1.

That was all down to geography, and the fact that many withdrawn Southern and Western locomotives ended up at Dai Woodham's Barry scrapyard.

There he stored them for many years while scrapping wagons instead, while locomotives from other regions went to works and breakers' yards where they were cut up within days of arrival. ■

Two preserved Bulleid Battle of Britain Pacifics back to back depart from Corfe Castle on the Swanage Railway on May 2, 2009. No. 34070 *Manston* leads visiting No. 34067 *Tangmere*.
ROBIN JONES

Bittern timed at 94

In parallel with the Mallard 75 events, special dispensation was given to one of the six surviving A4s to run three public trips at 90mph on the East Coast Main Line.

The locomotive was No. 4464 *Bittern*, and as highlighted in Mallard 75, the previous volume, the trips were organised by owner Jeremy Hosking's Locomotive Services in conjunction with Pathfinder Tours, backed by Network Rail engineers and Vehicle Acceptance Board inspectors.

The green light for the specials was given by Network Rail following the successful completion of high speed trials when *Bittern*, hauling eight coaches, achieved 90mph on former Western Region metals between Didcot and Reading on the early hours of May 29, 2013. The standard limit for steam locomotives on the main line today is 75mph.

The first of the three specials, the 'Ebor Streak', ran to schedule on June 29 – setting a new heritage era official speed

record of 92.5mph.

However, the following two high-speed runs, the 'Tyne-Tees Streak' and the 'Capital Streak', were cancelled due to Network Rail's summer fire risk steam ban.

Originally dated for July 19 and then rearranged in the first instance for August 30, the 'Tyne-Tees Streak' eventually ran on Thursday, December 5.

Departing Bristol Temple Meads for York behind DB Schenker Class 67 No. 67006, the

LNER A4 Pacific No. 4464 *Bittern* accelerates towards 90mph past Bolton Percy just south of York on December 7, 2013. PHIL WATERFIELD

'Tyne-Tees Streak' set out for York with 10 full coaches.

It was a day when the run-Pathfinder's train was again threatened by adverse weather conditions which had reduced all service train speeds working north of York to a maximum of 50mph because of storm force winds, strong enough to rock the station's footbridge

However, Network Rail came up trumps. Rather than postpone the train again because of the weather and the real risk of tree branches falling on to the wires, it was allowed to proceed.

The decision could not prevent the 'Tyne-Tees Streak' departing for Newcastle an hour late, partly due to the late running of a southbound train bringing *Bittern*'s driver to start his shift.

Passengers were certainly not disappointed by the performance of the A4, which worked the train from York to Newcastle and back.

The outward journey was affected by gales that severely depleted normal services and accordingly the train had to run at restricted speed.

The wind died down somewhat for the return leg, which was ambitiously scheduled to take 67 minutes for the 80.2 miles to York at an average timetabled speed of 71.8mph.

Maximum permissible speed derogations had been granted, easing the normal 75mph to 90mph for long stretches. Apart from slowing to 75mph for a bridge restriction at Northallerton, driver Steve Hanszar, fireman Keith Mufin and traction inspector Bob Hart combined to work the A4 up to 90mph for long periods.

ANOTHER NEW HERITAGE STEAM RECORD

There have been very few steam-hauled start-to-stop runs from Newcastle-York. The fastest was recorded in LNER days, in the form of a 1946 trial run with A4 No. 2512 *Silver Fox* on six coaches taking 68 minutes four seconds.

A GPS device in a passenger compartment on board the 'Tyne-Tees Streak' indicates 95mph on the return journey. However, it is recognised that all speed measuring devices used are subject to errors – including the mechanical variety in steam locomotives – and the figure could be several mph out. It is therefore highly unlikely that a GPS device would have been used by Gresley to record *Mallard*, instead of the equipment in the LNER dynamometer car, on July 3, 1938. Photographer John Turner said he saw the device show 96mph for a very short time before it fell back to 95mph.

Above: *Bittern* heads the December 7, 2013 'The Capital Streak' from York to King's Cross through East Markham (Gamston Summit) before undertaking 90mph running further south.
MICHAEL ANDERSON

The crew of LNER A4 Pacific No. 4464 *Bittern* in front of the engine shortly before departure from York on December 7, 2013. BRIAN SHARPE

With 10 coaches grossing around 370 tonnes, *Bittern* beat that record by 66 seconds by taking 66 minutes 58 seconds, according to *The Railway Magazine*'s practice and performance expert John Heaton, who was on board.

In the magazine's January 2014 issue, John wrote: "Some recorders have claimed the run to be another 38 seconds faster.

"There had been a hesitant start and possibly momentary halt, from which point some recorders adjusted their timings. If the train did indeed stop, and many at the rear of the train are doubtful, no doors were released and it was not subject to a second 'right-away', so it was in fact no different from any other form of delay en route."

Accelerating away from the permanent 85mph speed restriction at Aycliffe, speed crept towards the magic 90mph and hit 94mph on the 1-in-220 downgrade to Parkgate Junction. Passengers spontaneously applauded as the speed peaked.

The Thirsk to Tollerton leg showed an average of 91.2mph with a maximum of 92mph.

Locomotive Services Limited's general manager Richard Corser afterwards told *Heritage Railway* that the speed had peaked at 93mph.

Passenger John Turner, who was seated in the front coach, told the magazine that together with others he witnessed 95mph displayed on a tablet with a GPS speedometer app and photographed the screen for posterity. It has to be pointed out, however, that GPS devices have been challenged as to their accuracy.

The highlight of the run was on *Mallard*'s 1938 racing ground. John Heaton said: "After passing Grantham at 76.6mph, speed dropped to no lower than 71.16mph on the climb to Stoke summit, this time with 11 coaches and around 405 tonnes gross. After a compulsory slowing at Little Bytham, Bittern then took the 9.2 miles from Essendine to Werrington Junction at a flying average of 91.2mph with a maximum speed of 92mph."

John said: "It was a brilliant ride back from Newcastle to York and more than made up for the rather sedate 50mph limit demanded for the journey north earlier in the day."

MALLARD'S RACETRACK REVISITED

The 'Capital Streak', originally booked to run on July 27 and moved to August 31, finally ran on Saturday, December 7.

Bittern hauled the train from York to King's Cross with water stops at Retford and Conington South, and was again in sparkling form, running consistently at its 90mph.

The weather on the day was very different to that of the previous Thursday, as high winds had dropped and southbound services from York were back to normal.

With drivers Steve Hanszard and Mark Dale, fireman Dave Proctor and traction inspectors Gareth Jones and

Bittern stands at King's Cross after arriving with the 'Capital Streak' on December 7. PAUL SIMPSON

Colin Kerswill taking turns on the footplate, *Bittern* departed from York at 2.19pm with 11 full coaches behind the drawbar.

The A4 quickly accelerated to its normal line speed and then topped the 90mph mark after Doncaster racing towards Retford and Newark – where the 'Ebor Streak' was clocked at 92.5mph in June.

Of course, the highlight of the trips was the run over the section of track where *Mallard* achieved its 126mph, and which is now marked by a trackside sign.

John Heaton said: "After passing Grantham at 76½mph, speed dropped to no lower than 71½mph on the climb to Stoke summit, this time with 11 coaches and around 405 tonnes gross.

"After a compulsory slowing at Little Bytham, *Bittern* then took the 9.2 miles from Essendine to Werrington Junction at a flying average of 91.2mph with a maximum speed of 92mph."

Approaching the home straight, the 'Capital Streak' run was curtailed when a double yellow at Huntingdon and a 'feather' indicated that the train was being turned on to the Down slow line to let late running service trains pass.

Baulked by signals and slow line running, the train was reported arriving at King's Cross 36 minutes late – but did it matter?

Bittern's mission had been accomplished in style. It could be described only as a pulsating tribute to Sir Nigel Gresley's fleet of A4s.

However, it was not about breaking records. The two

90mph trains – the second ran on December 7 – was about showing that ageing but well-maintained steam locomotives are capable of holding their own on today's national network. ∎

RETFORD DEPART TO PETERBOROUGH PASS

Loco	A4 4-6-2 No. 4464 *Bittern*
Load	11/385/405
Train	14.19 York to King's Cross
Date	December 7 2013
Recorder	J. Heaton

Miles	Location	Sch	M. S.	M.P.H.
00.00	RETFORD d.	0	00 00	T
28.94	Barkston South Jct		26 42	73/70
30.25	PeasdiffeTNP		27 48	72/71
33.18	GRANTHAM	28'A	30 09	77
36.53	Great Ponton		32 52	73/71
38.86	Stoke Jct	33 Vi	34 47	73
41.46	Corby Glen		36 41	91/93/80
46.40	Little Bytham		40 02	82
49.91	Essendine		42 28	89
51.53	Greatford		43 32	92
53.81	Tallington	44½	45 02	92/91
56.71	Helpston		46 56	92/90
59.11	Werrington Jct		48 31	91/sigs 46
62.25	PETERBOROUGH	51	51 14	49

pass maximum whenever permitted to do so.

LNER A4 Pacific No. 4464 *Bittern* storms uphill through Grantham prior to topping Stoke summit at 72mph on December 7, 2013. DEREK PHILLIPS

It may not be 126mph, but the magic of A4 steam at high speed was relived as the 'Capital Streak' raced past the sign on Stoke Bank north of Essendine which marks *Mallard's* 1938 record. JOHN HILLIER

Above: LNER A4 Pacific No. 4464 *Bittern* heads north through Northallerton at around 30mph on Thursday, December 5, 2013. The southbound run under cover of darkness was faster. DEREK PHILLIPS

Left: So that's why they call it a Streak… yards from the Whistle Top pub, in failing light, Bittern thunders across the A16 at Tallington level crossing with the 'Capital Streak' on December 7, 2013. ROBIN JONES

Gone in a flash… a trail of smoke from Bittern forms a steam sculpture in the twilight above the 'Capital Streak'. JOHN HILLIER

CHAPTER ELEVEN

The rebirth of 'The Cross'

It was from the great 'cathedral of steam', London's King's Cross station, that the A4s set out for the Scottish capital, cutting the journey time to little over four hours, and as we have seen, setting the odd record in the process.

While the world's attention was on Mallard 75 and the Great Gatherings, the finishing touches were being added to a £550 million scheme to take this magnificent terminus, the spiritual home of the Gresley Pacifics, into the 21st century and beyond.

Following the award-winning transformation of the Midland Railway's London terminus next door into St Pancras International, handling trains to Paris and Brussels via the Channel Tunnel, 'the Cross' was next on the upgrade list.

Not before time too. For decades, the King's Cross area had been regarded as one of the less salubrious parts of London, the haunt of prostitutes, drug dealers and users and a host of other ne-er do wells. Yet, it is one of the busiest transport interchanges in the country. Around 47 million passengers use the station every year, a number expected to rise by 10 million by 2023.

However, a real-life rags-to-riches tale has unfolded. The regeneration of the district, with the station at its heart, has created one of the most desirable areas of the capital for the relocation of businesses, and the great

terminus will again do London justice as one of its primary gateways, just as in the days when the A4s reigned supreme.

The redevelopment of the station, undertaken by Network Rail in partnership with English Heritage, at the core of the district has helped to attract £2.2 billion of private investment into a previously largely derelict and disused 67-acre site, with 2000 new homes.

Designed by Lewis Cubitt, another member of the great family of civil engineers, King's Cross station was built during 1851–52 on the site of a former smallpox hospital, superseding a temporary terminus at Maiden Lane north of the Regent's Canal, which had been opened on August 7, 1850 in time for the Great Exhibition the following year.

The initial blueprint for the station was drawn up in 1848 by George Turnbull, resident engineer for construction of the first 20 miles of the Great Northern railway running northwards from the capital. However, Lewis Cubitt produced the detailed design.

King's Cross, formerly Battle Bridge, takes its name from a monument to King George IV that was built near the spot, at the junction of Gray's Inn Road, Pentonville Road and New Road (later Euston Road). Standing 60ft tall with an 11ft statue of the monarch on top, it

LNER A4 Pacific No. 60009 *Union of South Africa* awaits departure from King's Cross with the Railway Touring Company's 'York Yuletide Express' on December 14, 2013. No. 60009 returned to main line action after the Autumn Great Gathering with the RTC's 'Tynesider' one way from Newcastle to King's Cross on November 30. It also headed RTC tours to York from Cambridge, Norwich and King's Cross over the following three weeks before returning north with a one-way run from Victoria to York via the Midland Main Line on December 21. CHRIS BOYD

The roof of King's Cross, now covered in photovoltaic panel glazing, with cranes to the left on the horizon highlighting the major redevelopment of a once very rundown part of the capital. ROBIN JONES

A4 No. 60022 *Mallard* about to depart from King's Cross with the 'Aberdeen Flyer' on June 2, 1962. COLOUR-RAIL

The refurbished clock tower above the Lewis Cubitt façade. ROBIN JONES

The exterior of King's Cross station in late Victorian times. ENGLISH HERITAGE

The interior of the stylish modern Western Concourse which adjoins the original fabric of the structure of the station, but does not disfigure it. ROBIN JONES

was completed in the mid-1830s. The bottom housed an exhibition space, police station and later a beer shop. Never a popular edifice, it was demolished in 1845, and lives on in name only.

The main part of King's Cross station, which today includes Platforms 1 to 8, was opened on October 14, 1852. At first there was only one arrival and one departure platform, which survive today at Platforms 1 and 8, with carriage sidings taking up the space in-between.

Lewis Cubitt's magnificent façade at the buffer-stops end of the trainshed is a splendid piece of architecture that in his day and for decades after could not fail to impress.

However, as the station became busier and expanded to cope with ever-increasing demand in the 20th century, many of the historical features were 'lost' – buried behind later 'improvements', covered up by characterless additions or simply painted over. The most glaring example being British Rail's 1972 'lean to' which completed the despoiling of the view of the façade.

This single-storey utilitarian extension was built on to the front of the station to contain the main passenger concourse and ticket office, obscuring the façade to a far greater extent than before. Previously, it was hidden behind a small terrace of shops.

The redevelopment programme followed the spirit of that carried out on St Pancras to the immediate west. Rather than sweep away the last vestiges of the past, the approach taken by the architects was to uncover them once again, and restore them to their full glory, while adapting the fabric of the building to

An aerial view of the two great London termini: St Pancras International (left) and King's Cross (right). NETWORK RAIL

serve the needs of the modern passenger.

The project began in 2007. One of the first phases saw Network Rail build a new platform, Platform 0. Then the old eastern and western range offices, which run the length of the station, were restored.

The historic Handyside bridge, which spanned the tracks in the middle of the station, was replaced by an accessible footbridge. The Handyside bridge has been relocated to Ropley on the Mid-Hants Railway: indeed, heritage features not used in the facelift of the station were offered to preservation groups elsewhere, as part of a recycling programme of artefacts. For decades, the interior of the trainshed had been considered gloomy, a fact that the tens of millions of passengers who use it took for granted for so long that nobody ever complained.

Now, following the replacement of the glass roofing windows with photovoltaic panels, which generate solar energy, the natural light has returned with a vengeance. These panels even generate 10% of the station's energy requirements.

Furthermore, a new 75,000sq ft public open space, King's Cross Square, designed by architects Stanton Williams, has been laid out in front of the Grade I listed station's façade.

In 2012, King's Cross station welcomed the opening of a new space-age style western concourse, a modern addition grafted on to the re-exposed heritage fabric on the western walls of the original station and containing retail outlets and restaurants. Since this new concourse opened, passenger satisfaction at the station soared by 33%.

Now the 'new' King's Cross has regained its rightful place as one of London's landmark buildings, just as in the days of the LNER and its predecessor the Great Northern Railway.

John McAslan, chairman of John McAslan + Partners, added: "We are very proud of our role

(plaque reads:) ENGLISH HERITAGE / SIR NIGEL GRESLEY / 1876-1941 / Locomotive Engineer / had his office / in this station / 1923-1941

INSET: The blue plaque highlights the fact that A4 designer Sir Nigel Gresley had his office at King's Cross between 1923-41. Was it here that many of his design ideas came together? ROBIN JONES

View over the King's Cross platforms in the Sixties. JOHN GAY/ENGLISH HERITAGE

The unsightly 1972 'lean to' structure obscured the façade, and considered unanimously to be of no architectural merit, was removed in 2013. ROBIN JONES

as lead architects and master-planners of the King's Cross redevelopment.

"This project has been a complex, extraordinary and collaborative effort that has delivered an internationally significant transport interchange, fit for the 21st century and beyond."

Alan Stanton, director of Stanton Williams, said: "As architects, we were delighted to work on King's Cross Square and to develop a response to one of the most exciting urban challenges in the city. The design of this unique new public space takes into account all the complexities of the site, from its function as an arrivals concourse for the station, to the structures of the London Underground system

below, to create a welcoming orientation and meeting space, as the final step to the regeneration of this landmark station."

Secretary of state for transport, Patrick McLoughlin, the Mayor of London Boris Johnson and Network Rail chief executive Sir David Higgins declared the new King's Cross Square officially open, at a ceremony on September 26, 2013. The occasion was marked by the pulling of a Victorian railway signal lever and an explosion of streamer cannons.

Mr McLoughlin said: "I have been travelling to and from my Derbyshire constituency for years and I remember when King's Cross and St Pancras were not places you would hang around. Now it is a destination in its own right.

"The official opening of King's Cross Square marks the completion of one of the largest station modernisation projects across our national rail network and one of the government's top infrastructure projects. With more platforms, a redesigned concourse and improved facilities, work at this iconic station has transformed the experience of thousands of rail passengers travelling into London for the better.

"It has also been the catalyst for one of the largest regeneration schemes in Europe."

Boris Johnson added: "The transformation of King's Cross is not only beautiful but it has also triggered all sorts of regeneration, with new jobs, huge numbers of homes being built and businesses relocating here. What has emerged is a fantastic open space which has led to the creation of a whole new vibrant district.

"It is the perfect example of a point I have always made, if you support good transport links the jobs and growth will follow."

David Higgins said: "I'm confident King's Cross will continue to flourish. This is just the beginning of a new chapter."

And yes, the splendid 'new' terminus is still being graced by surviving examples of the most strikingly beautiful locomotives to pull up alongside its platforms in the steam era – Gresley's 'Streaks'.

A4 No. 4464 *Bittern* stands in Platform 1 with the 'Cathedrals Express' on June 17, 2013. JOHN TITLOW

The new western entrance to the refurbished King's Cross. ROBIN JONES

The latest bird to appear at King's Cross is not a bittern, golden plover, golden snipe or osprey, but a Harris Hawk. And she's watching your every move!

While the new showpiece western concourse is definitely 21st century in design, some of its pest control methods hark back to before the dawn of steam.

Pestokill, a firm specialising in railway pest control, uses Denise, a Harris Hawk, to control the number of pigeons inside the concourse.

Like the rest of her species, Denise is able to catch and kill an errant pigeon within minutes. However, her handler never lets her off his arm. No need – the mere sight of Denise is sufficient to make the pigeons leave quicker than *Mallard* could descend Stoke Bank!

So Denise earns her keep and the pigeons live to fly another day; outside.

Formerly known as the bay-winged hawk or dusky hawk, the Harris Hawk (*Parabuteo unicinctus*) was named by naturalist John James Audubon in honour of his ornithological companion, financial supporter, and friend Edward Harris. ROBIN JONES

CHAPTER TWELVE

Giants
of the
Roundhouse

No 4464
CLASS A4

When Steve Davies and his team at the National Railway Museum reached agreement to borrow the two A4s from North America, it was on the understanding that the pair would not be displayed at other venues.

However, once they were over here, Barrow Hill Roundhouse, which had built up a solid track record of classic events including line-ups of LNER locomotives even though it is deep within LMS territory, was granted special dispensation by the US National Railroad Museum and Exporail to borrow No. 4489 *Dominion of Canada* and No. 60008 *Dwight D. Eisenhower* for a one-off event.

Titled East Coast Giants, more than 6000 people turned up over the weekend of February 8-9 2014, when the weather proved better than expected. Much of the rest of Britain was suffering from freak levels of rain and wind which had left large parts of southern England underwater.

The big appeal of Barrow Hill, as far as the expatriate A4s was concerned, was that it presented the only chance to view and photograph them in a classic working engine shed and rail yard setting, as opposed to a museum venue.

The pair were lined up alongside A2 No. 60532 *Blue Peter* in the Roundhouse yard, with No. 4464 *Bittern*, which

hauled passenger trains up the venue's Springwell branch, making regular appearances in the line-up. Meanwhile, new-build Peppercorn A1 Pacific No. 60163 *Tornado*, undergoing planned annual maintenance at the Roundhouse, attracted much attention in its prime position on the turntable.

Class 55 Deltic D9009 *Alycidon*, one of the successors to the Gresley Pacifics at the end of East Coast Main Line steam, welcomed visitors to the show on display on the Roundhouse bay platform, while sister No. 55019 *Royal Highland Fusilier* completed the powerful line-up in the Deltic Preservation Society's depot.

Night show: A4s No. 4464 Bittern, No. 4489 *Dominion of Canada* and No. 60008 *Dwight D. Eisenhower* at Russ Hillier and Geoff Silcock's Sentimental Journeys' evening photo charter on February 7. JOHN TITLOW

Nº 4489
CLASS A4

Above: *Dominion of Canada* in the slow lane on the A64 Tadcaster bypass en route from the National Railway Museum York to Barrow Hill. DAVID B TILLOTSON.

Below: The Barrow Hill Giants of Steam line-up: A4 No. 4464 *Bittern*, A2 No. 60532 *Blue Peter* and A4s No. 4489 *Dominion of Canada* and No. 60008 *Dwight D. Eisenhower,* pictured on February 7. ROBIN JONES

The event began with a private photo charter on Thursday, February 6, followed on the Friday by a VIP and press preview day which welcomed representatives from all sectors of the railway world including main line train operating companies, the National Railway Museum, heritage railways and preservation societies.

The preview was also attended by representatives of Derbyshire County Council and Chesterfield Borough Council.

David Horne, managing director of East Midlands Trains, was on hand to welcome one of the company's High Speed Train sets, headed in to the Barrow Hill platform by Class 43 No. 43050 with No. 43046 on the rear, on a special rail tour charter which brought 450 people from London to the event.

Richard Corser, general manager of Locomotive Services Ltd, which manages *Bittern*, was assisted by Alexa Stott from the Roundhouse in unveiling a plaque on *Bittern*, commemorating the locomotive's three historic 90mph passenger-carrying runs in 2013 in honour of *Mallard's* world speed for steam record.

However, surely the proudest person there was Tim Godfrey, grandson of Sir Nigel Gresley, who brought along his grandfather's hat.

Dominion of Canada and *Dwight D. Eisenhower* being towed from the NRM by Class 37 No. 37518 on January 28, with Deltic No. 55002 *King's Own Light Infantry* tailing behind. The pair were given a short licence by Network Rail to be towed out on the main line to York Wagon Works, where they were later loaded on to low loaders to be transported to Barrow Hill Roundhouse. NRM

IN 2013 THIS LOCOMOTIVE UNDERTOOK THREE 90 MPH RUNS TO HONOUR MALLARD'S WORLD SPEED RECORD OF 1938

BITTERN

Watched by Locomotive Services Ltd general manager Richard Corser, Barrow Hill's Alexa Stott unveils the plaque on *Bittern* which marks the locomotive's heritage-era steam speed record set in 2013. ROBIN JONES

Dwight D. Eisenhower was the first of the two A4s to arrive at Barrow Hill on January 28, where it is seen in the Roundhouse. MERVYN ALLCOCK

Despite the heavy rain elsewhere, the sun shone on Barrow Hill for most of the weekend, enabling visitors who had travelled from all corners of the UK to get many great photographs and videos of this once-in-a-lifetime event.

While attention was focused on the A4s, there were many other attractions, including the sight of the unique Vulcan Foundry industrial 0-4-0ST *Vulcan* hauling brake van rides in the yard, assisted by the venue's Class 03 shunter.

The OO gauge layout, Grantham: the Streamliner Years, was a popular exhibit in the Roundhouse and during the course of the weekend ran models of all 35 original LNER A4s in celebration of the visit of the transatlantic A4s.

Meanwhile, in the Deltic Preservation Society depot, people were able to visit the cab of *Royal Highland Fusilier* and see the other OO gauge layout, Deepcar, running models of all the Deltics.

The two A4s departed Barrow Hill after the event, in the same way that they had arrived – by road. Moveright International, which had orchestrated their marathon move across North America and the Atlantic, took them to their last show in the UK, the Great Goodbye at Shildon. ∎

Matlock couple Neal and Julia Garratt won the whistle carried by A4 No. 4464 *Bittern* during its three public 90mph runs in 2013, in a special prize draw. The couple, passengers on the second trip, were presented with the whistle by *Bittern* operator Locomotive Services Ltd manager Richard Corser (left) at the VIP day at Barrow Hill on Friday, February 7. ROBIN JONES

Above: Great Northern Railway C1 class 4-4-0 No. 251 was on static display outside the Roundhouse during the event. It may well be considered a beginning of the A4 story, for it was Henry Ivatt's Atlantics that began the GNR's large-boilered engine policy. The C1 class was designed as a powerful free-steaming locomotive capable of heading the GNR's fastest and heaviest express trains, sometimes weighing more than 500 tonnes. No. 251 was the first of them, appearing in 1902, with 80 more built at Doncaster between 1904 and 1908. Gresley drew up plans for a longer version of the Ivatt Atlantic in 1915, but found his four-cylinder design unsatisfactory. He then looked at the Pennsylvania Railroad's new K4 Pacific, the final evolution of a series of prototypes produced in 1910-11, and was sufficiently inspired to build a modern steam locomotive for Britain. The design for his Pacifics exploited the maximum limits of the East Coast Main Line loading gauge with large boilers and wide fireboxes providing a large grate area. His first two Pacifics appeared in 1922, No. 1470 *Great Northern* and No. 1471 *Sir Frederick Banbury*. They led to the building of the A1s, later A3s, and the rest is history. ROBIN JONES

Below: *Bittern, Blue Peter, Dominion of Canada* and *Dwight D. Eisenhower* pictured during the February 6 photo charter. JOHN TITLOW

BARROW HILL
ROUNDHOUSE

Built in 1870 Barrow Hill's roundhouse was threatened with demolition in 1991 when the site was closed by British Rail. It was saved by a group of dedicated volunteers who have transformed it into a premier railway venue. It is the last surviving railway roundhouse in the UK with an operational turntable.
ROBIN JONES

The giants in profile: *Dwight D. Eisenhower, Dominion of Canada* and *Bittern*. ROBIN JONES

The driver leaves the cab of *Dwight D. Eisenhower* on the evening of February 6. DUNCAN LANGTREE

Among the guests at the February 7 preview day was Tim Godfrey, grandson of Sir Nigel Gresley. He is pictured (centre) the week before at an event along another example of his grandfather's work, the Severn Valley Railway's 1943-built LNER Gresley-designed Gangwayed Brake Pigeon Van, rolled out for the benefit of supporters at Bewdley station after the vehicle's new roof was completed. Either side of Tim, who is holding Sir Nigel's hat, are Nick Paul CBE, chairman of Severn Valley Railway (Holdings) plc and David McIntosh, chairman of the Gresley Society Trust. SVR

Above: The loco crew wish their charges, *Bittern* and *Dominion of Canada*, goodnight on February 6. MATTHEW TOMS

Left: Framed by steam: during the Giants of Steam event, *Bittern*, the only operational A4 on site, gave short rides along Barrow Hill's Springwell branch. ROBIN JONES

Mallard: The Magnificent Six 99

It could so easily be Haymarket, New England or even King's Cross' Top Shed: *Bittern* is checked over on the evening on February 6. DUNCAN LANGTREE

The moment that the 35th A4 ran on the Grantham layout during the weekend. The noticeboard behind them recorded all their workings. GRAHAM NICHOLAS Inset: The line-up of OO scale A4s belonging to The A1 Steam Locomotive Trust chairman Mark Allatt. At no stage were 35 together in the line-up, as up to six were running around the layout.

Nose to nose: the incoming East Midlands Trains' HST charter comes face-to-face with No. 4464 *Bittern* in the Barrow Hill yard on February 7. The venue is connected to the national network and this has encouraged several commercial rail companies to base their activities at Barrow Hill, generating more than 40 jobs and making a valuable contribution to the local economy. Clients include Network Rail, DRS, Freightliner, GBRf, Colas, BARS, West Coast Railways, Venice Simplon Orient-Express, the Harry Needle Railroad Company, NewRail (the railway research facility affiliated to Newcastle University), Rampart and Intertrain. ROBIN JONES

CHAPTER THIRTEEN

The electric 'Mallard'!

The same weekend that crowds packed Barrow Hill to see *Bittern*, *Dwight D. Eisenhower* and *Dominion of Canada* line up, another East Coast Main Line record holder was returning to action.

In this case, it was Class 91 electric locomotive No. 91110, which had just undergone a major servicing programme, carried out by Wabtec Rail Limited in Doncaster. This locomotive's claim to fame came on September 17, 1989, just over half a century after *Mallard*'s exploits, when numbered 91010, it set a British locomotive speed record at 162mph which still stands today. The feat was achieved – where else – but down Stoke Bank, just south of Little Bytham, with the Class 225 set's Driving Van Trailer leading.

Today's equivalent of the express trains hauled by the A4s, the Class 225 units entered service in 1990 following electrification of the ECML. Each set comprises Class 91 locomotive, nine Mk.4 coaches and a Driving Van Trailer. The Class 91 locomotives were built by British Rail Engineering Limited at Crewe Works as a spin-off from the Advanced Passenger Train project, which was abandoned during the 1980s. The 225s were designed to operate at up to 140mph in regular service, but limited to 125mph due to a lack of cab signalling.

No. 91110 carries the name *Battle of Britain Memorial Flight*, in honour of the famous fleet of Second World War aeroplanes operating from RAF Coningsby in Lincolnshire. It was dedicated to the flight on June 2, 2012, the opening day of the National Railway Museum's nine-day Railfest 2012 event – in the presence of none other than *Mallard* itself.

The ceremony began with individual flypasts by the Spitfire, Hurricane and Lancaster aircraft in the run-up to the train naming by Carol Vorderman. The three planes then formed up and flew together over the stage as Carol unveiled the East Coast locomotive in its commemorative livery.

Its nameplates, when unveiled, appeared to be very much inspired by those carried by Bulleid's Battle of Britain's Light Pacifics on the Southern Railway.

The logo on the front of the 91 features the three aircraft plus the Royal Air Force roundel, RAF BBMF insignia and Lest We Forget motto. The locomotive also carries a pair of 'oak leaf' cast-iron plates commemorating its record-holding status, in similar style to those carried by *Mallard*.

At the ceremony, East Coast director of communications Paul Emberley said: "Bestowing the Battle of Britain Memorial Flight name on this electric locomotive is highly appropriate, and the commemorative plates kindly donated by the NRM will continue to emphasise the power and prestige of the East Coast route – just as Sir Nigel Gresley's streamlined locomotive *Mallard* did in the steam age."

Following the 2014 refit, East Coast managing director Karen Boswell said: "This locomotive has won a special place in the hearts of our staff and passengers alike, and after 19 months' hard work on our long-distance services, we're delighted that it has been fully refreshed and rededicated for further service.

"As the finishing touches were made to No. 91110, a brief ceremony of rededication and blessing for the locomotive was conducted by the railway chaplain, Rev Dr Stephen Sorby, watched by representatives from Wabtec

The Battle of Britain Memorial Flight swoops above world steam record holder No. 4468 *Mallard* following the naming of Class 91 No. 91110 by Carol Vorderman on June 2 during the National Railway Museum's Railfest 2012 event. ROBIN JONES

Above: Class 91 No. 91110 at the National Railway Museum following its dedication on June 2, 2012. ROBIN JONES

Reunited with Class 91 No. 91110 at the official opening of Railfest 2012 were drivers Ken Humphrey and John Swaby, who were at the controls on September 17, 1989, when it followed in the tracks of *Mallard* by setting a new British locomotive speed record on Stoke Bank. ROBIN JONES

The ceremony of rededication and blessing for No. 91110 at Wabtec. EAST COAST

Engineering, East Coast and the RAF BBMF. Among them was Sqn Ldr Stuart Reid (retired) who flew the BBMF's Lancaster bomber for the last 11 years of his career, and who first suggested the locomotive naming.

He said: "This locomotive takes one of the key messages of the RAF BBMF along the East Coast Main Line – to recognise and commemorate the selfless acts of bravery of over 100,000 RAF airmen and airwomen who have defended our freedom over decades, many making the ultimate sacrifice.

"The teams at East Coast and Wabtec, and the livery's designer Paul Gentleman, have done an excellent job in ensuring that this special locomotive will continue to turn heads, including in Lincolnshire where many of the 55,573 men of Bomber Command took the offensive to Germany and never returned. This record-holding loco is a fitting symbol in honour of them all." ∎

Britain's fastest locomotive, Class 91 No. 91110, is given a final polish before returning to traffic in February 2014. EAST COAST

The Great
Goodbye

Alongside part of the world's first public steam railway, the Stockton & Darlington, six locomotives representing the zenith of British express passenger steam locomotive design in this dramatic night-time view from the February 17 evening photographic charter. DAVE HEWITT

The town of Shildon in County Durham owes its existence to railways. Already a centre of the booming local coal mining industry of the 18th and early 19th centuries which was served by a network of horse-drawn wagonways, it was there in 1825 that the Stockton & Darlington Railway opened its workshops. On September 27 that year, the first public passenger train ran over what was the world's first steam-operated public railway.

Many of the early pioneer steam locomotives such as Timothy Hackworth's *Sans Pareil* were built at the workshops. The railway owned much of the surrounding land and little Shildon mushroomed in size to having a population of around 9000. Indeed, it is with total justification

that the town became known as the 'cradle of the railways'.

After the Second World War, Shildon had one of the biggest sidings complexes in Europe and was established as a major centre for wagon building. However, in 1984 the wagon works closed, ending a proud legacy that had begun in the days of George and Robert Stephenson.

Nine years earlier, a major cavalcade of historic locomotives and modern traction led by a replica of the Stockton & Darlington *Locomotion No. 1* was held on August 31, 1975, to mark the 150th anniversary of the Stockton & Darlington Railway. That was the same year in which the National Railway Museum at York was opened, combining the

earlier York Railway Museum and the British Transport Museum at Clapham.

In 2004, a purpose-designed branch of the NRM was opened alongside the route of the Stockton & Darlington Railway at Shildon by local MP and then prime minister Tony Blair, affording valuable under cover storage to National Collection vehicles for which there was no space at York. Its extensive site includes the former Timothy Hackworth Museum, which contains the original Sans Pareil, and the inventor's home.

Named Locomotion: The National Railway Museum at Shildon, it was designed to accommodate 60,000 visitors a year.

As is the case at the NRM in York, under

government policy admission is free.

The museum was from the start more successful than anyone had dared hope, as visitor numbers exceeded original estimates.

However, a new all-time high was reached during the February 15-23, 2014, schhol half-term week when thanks to its impeccable railway pedigree, all eyes were once again focused on Shildon.

Public steam railways began with the likes of *Sans Pareil* and Stephenson's *Rocket*, but in many ways reached a summit when *Mallard* set an all-time world steam speed record well over a century later. It was therefore appropriate that the last of the three Mallard 75 Great Gatherings was staged at Locomotion.

The man who made it happen: former National Railway Museum director Steve Davies made several visits to the Great Goodbye. ANTHONY COULLS

MORE NATIONAL ACCLAIM

It's a winner! Tobias Lumb, senior project manager at the National Railway Museum and manager of the Mallard 75 project, receives the Heritage Railway Association's 2013 John Coiley Award for Locomotive Projects from the organisation's president Lord Faulkner of Worcester at its annual awards presentation evening at the Guildhall in Bath on February 8, 2014.

The award to the NRM acknowledged and celebrated the international co-operation and achievement of the transatlantic partners in the movement of *Dominion of Canada* and *Dwight D. Eisenhower* to take part in Mallard 75. This involved major input from the Friends of the National Railway Museum, the museum itself and all the groups whose generosity made the move possible, particularly haulier Moveright International.

The citation said that the operation would not have been possible without the unstinting support of Exporail: The Canadian Railway Museum and the National Railroad Museum in the USA.
GWYNN JONES/HRA

Mallard being cleaned inside the Locomotion main building on February 6, the day after its arrival for the last gathering. LOCOMOTION

BEYOND ANYONE'S WILDEST DREAMS

Sixty thousand visitors a year? That figure was passed at the Great Goodbye during the first five days of the nine-day event – by the end of which a total of 119,880 visitors had passed through the doors to pay homage to the unique outdoor line-ups of British transport technology's art deco finest.

By contrast, the museum's best visitor attendance for an event was recorded in 2010, when new-build A1 Peppercorn Pacific No. 60163 *Tornado* was displayed for four days. That event attracted 21,000 visitors.

In February 2014, however, sleepy Shildon was yanked back into life. If anyone had forgotten about its rich railway past, they were reminded with a jolt.

On roads approaching the Locomotion museum car parks, tailbacks of traffic well over a mile built up as crowds flocked in the February sunshine to see the A4s, climb on to their footplates, or take a brakevan ride behind one of the legendary giants of steam.

Northern Rail, which runs services on the Darlington to Bishop Auckland branch, part of the original Stockton & Darlington Railway, introduced extra trains for the duration of the Great Goodbye, upping the frequency from two hourly to one, and doubling them in size from two-car Class 142 diesel multiple sets to twin-set rakes. Still it was barely enough, as many of the trains were packed to standing room only.

Locomotion officials had 'guesstimated' an attendance of around 70,000 for the week. By

The afternoon of Wednesday, February 5, 2014, saw *Union of South Africa* towing *Mallard* from the National Railway Museum at York along the East Coast Main Line to the Locomotion museum. STUART BROWN

the second day, it was clear that this figure was way wide of the mark. By the Sunday, lengthy queues of visitors tailed back from the entrance as staff were forced to limit the number of admissions due to fire regulations. However, those waiting in the queue for an hour or more still had a grandstand view not only of the A4s but also of No. 4464 *Bittern* hauling short brakevan rides along the museum's internal running line.

Trade boomed in the town throughout the event. One pub reported a boost in takings of 300%. Another which normally served 100 meals a week saw the figure rise to more than 250.

For the day events, the six A4s were not lined up evenly as had been the case at York. Five of them were arranged on the museum yard apron in a staggered formation, in order to place large wooden steps alongside them to allow cab access to visitors.

From the moment the doors opened at 9.30am each day to closing time at 5pm, endless queues of people wanting to 'cab' an A4 formed alongside each of the five.

Each day, one of the three operation A4s would offer brakevan trips from the museum platform, so did not form part of the line-up on the apron.

However, a series of midweek evening enthusiast photographic charters at £90-a-head was held, at which all six A4s were lined up together on the apron.

Solihull-based Martin Creese of 30742 Charters was brought in by Locomotion to organise the events, which were quickly sold out.

The rain which had caused extensive flooding in many parts of England during the preceding weeks luckily held off and the bumper attendances showed no sign of abating. On the final Saturday, more than 18,000 visitors turned up.

An hour before the doors opened on a wet February 15, all six A4s are lined up in their public display positions on the Locomotion museum apron. ANTHONY COULLS

The operational A4s took turns on different days during the Great Goodbye offering public brakevan rides along the Locomotion running line. Sunday, February 16, saw No. 4464 *Bittern* in action. BRIAN SHARPE

THAT MAN MALLARD!

Driver Percy Elcoat worked for the LNER's main rival, the LMS. Yet he was so enamoured of *Mallard* that he decided to name his son after the world record breaker.

Percy told his wife Ethel that when they had a child, he wanted to name the baby after the 'Streak'.

Ethel was not overly impressed, but gave in provided he had the more usual David as a middle name.

However, when he was tired of being the butt of duck jokes at school and as a teenager, young Mallard switched his names around to David Mallard Elcoat and it has stayed that way ever since.

Now 63, on Monday, February 18, he was united with his mechanical namesake at Locomotion during the Great Goodbye and brought his birth certificate along.

Mallard on board *Mallard*: Mallard David Elcoat meets his namesake: LOCOMOTION

He said: "I am extremely proud of my unusual name which always received a lot of interest. However, in my late teens I was getting quite a bit of banter about it and that's when I decided to adopt the use of David – my mother wasn't very happy about this. My wife also frequently reminds me that I should be proud of my birth name.

"I am a coach driver and over more recent years I have started to tell people about the story of my name when I take them round – and they are always keen to listen.

"I am so pleased that I am able to be part of the event and come to the museum to see the A4s; not surprisingly I am a bit of a rail enthusiast myself and it was an amazing opportunity for myself and many others. I was proud to stand next to *Mallard* at the museum."

Sarah Towers, marketing communications officer at Locomotion, said: "So many people feel a personal connection with the locomotives and this is another interesting story linked to the A4s."

Museum manager Dr George Muirhead said: "The project has brought us so many interesting stories about how these engines have influenced people in so many different ways. It is brilliant that we have been able to work with these international icons and it has been an excellent opportunity for the museum, County Durham and the North East region."

WHY DID WE DO IT?

One of the big highlights of the Great Goodbye was the public Mallard 75 gala dinner which was held at Locomotion on the evening of Friday, February 21.

Introduced by current National Railway Museum head Paul Kirkman, who oversaw the Mallard 75 year of celebrations, the guest speaker was none other than the man who dreamed up the whole affair, his predecessor Steve Davies.

He said: "What we have witnessed has been remarkable from whichever angle you view it. Visitor number records have been blown out of the water; significant retail and commercial revenue streams have given a major financial shot in the arm to the York and Shildon operations, and to the Science Museum Group as a whole; the national and international press have lavished the NRM with unprecedented levels of positive coverage; royal and High Commissioner-level patronage has provided a rich coating of gloss and gravitas to events; the world's enthusiasts have flocked to the NRM's door, the most distant from a South Pacific island; and most importantly the event has been fun.

"But why did we do it? What possible reason could there be for a nation to go all dewy-eyed about six large lumps of metal with pointy fronts, as a non-enthusiast friend of mine put it? How could the mere act of gathering together the last six lucky survivors of the most aesthetically pleasing class of steam locomotive ever built create such a riot of enthusiasm and delight?

"Well the reasons are not hard to find if you possess an understanding of the psyche of the British people.

"We are a race which loves our railways. We

The yard at Shildon on the second day of the Great Goodbye, with *Bittern* in steam (left) and the other five lined up in front of the museum building. BRIAN SHARPE

love to complain about them too – but we love them all the same. We like nothing better than to enjoy a jolly good commemoration, preferably really historic, and if it is to celebrate something that we as a nation are immensely proud of, so much the better.

"*Mallard*'s record breaking anniversary therefore had to be celebrated. But the 75th birthday called for something seriously imaginative, particularly as there was no prospect of the locomotive being returned to traffic for the event. At a time of national austerity, perhaps the country needed a lift; to be reminded of its considerable engineering achievements? Perhaps our contemporary modern railway network needed a celebratory event around which it could fully unite with the railway heritage movement? Or then again, was it a time for the National Railway Museum to demonstrate its world-leading status, and to employ its corporate and reputational muscle to make something very special happen? These and many other motives were present to varying degrees throughout the project.

"But whatever the motives, this has nevertheless been a project which fundamentally flew on the back of an innate gut instinct that the sheer audacity of assembling all six surviving A4s would capture the public imagination.

"There was no market-tested analysis involved; no focus groups proposing risk-free but bland compromise solutions; no business case looking at the commercial viability of such an operation; and certainly no fall-back plan in the event that sponsorship was not forthcoming.

"No, this was a project that depended for success on a compellingly articulated vision which potential sponsors and supporters alike

would feel instinctively drawn to. A vision that the overseas organisations involved would feel they did not wish to miss out on. A vision which was clear that this seminal anniversary should become a vehicle to reach out to the overwhelmingly non-enthusiast majority of this country. And a vision that would be driven through to successful completion regardless of the challenges and its detractors.

TRANSATLANTIC SUCCESS

"The fact that two of the locomotives involved were on the other side of the Atlantic simply added to the project's

attractive complexity. Who will ever forget the sense of escalating dramatic expectation as the locomotives concerned undertook their complex journey from foreign shores back to their country of birth? We were all frustratingly hungry for information, rather like an expectant father being ordered to sit in the waiting room during the delivery of his first-born.

"Let's be clear – it was the transatlantic dimension that made Mallard 75 the success that it has become. If all six locomotives had been based in the UK, then the 'mission impossible' nature of Mallard 75 would have been seriously diluted.

Bidding their final farewell: a group of former A4 locomen from Doncaster and King's Cross sheds were special guests at Locomotion on February 22, the penultimate day of the Great Gathering. LOCOMOTION

Photographers vie with each other on the ever-crowded museum apron to take a picture of as many A4s as they can with the fewest people possible! ROBIN JONES

The Mallard 75 logo was projected on to the walls of 11th century Durham Castle on the evening of Monday, February 3, 2014, announcing the Great Goodbye at Shildon. NRM

"Future reunions would always have been viewed as a possibility, so it was this never-to-be-repeated aspect of the project which was eventually to become the main reason for its success.

"Although much focus has been on *Dwight D. Eisenhower* and *Dominion of Canada;* paradoxically the most important first step in organising Mallard 75 was not to approach our opposite numbers in Green Bay and Montreal, but to write confidentially to the private owners of *Sir Nigel Gresley, Union of South Africa* and *Bittern* outlining the plan, swearing them to secrecy, and asking for their agreement to take part. For if only one of them had declined then the whole point of the exercise would have been defeated and it

would have been pointless even discussing the matter with our North American allies.

"I am delighted to report that they all replied in the affirmative by return of post, and kept the project a closely guarded secret despite the many discussions and meetings we held to pull the programme together. *Mallard*'s participation as a nationally owned asset was a given, but I think we should be collectively grateful that the private owners of the UK-based A4s so readily took part in the celebrations with what must have been an impact on their respective income streams. They shared the vision and helped make it a reality, and I believe we should now show our appreciation in time-honoured fashion.

THE HEROES OF MALLARD 75

"Ambitious plans need a sprinkling of heroes to make them happen. This story is no different. It was heroic of the National Railroad Museum, Green Bay, and Exporail, the Canadian Railway Museum in Montreal, to entrust their precious locomotives to the care of the National Railway Museum in the first place. Their response to my initial phone call was cautiously positive, but they subsequently very enthusiastically hosted the many technical visits which were necessary to get this complex project off the ground.

"Both museums were quick to grasp the potential benefits for their respective international profiles of joining us in this venture and I hope they feel that they have reaped a significant reward in this respect.

"The Friends of the National Railway Museum were equally heroic in trusting their instincts and investing in the cosmetic restoration of our transatlantic visitors.

"The promise to cosmetically restore the locomotives on arrival in the UK was a key incentive in negotiating the loans, and I breathed a huge sigh of relief when the Friends Council agreed the £50,000 needed. I gather, though, that their investment has been turned into a healthy profit in retail sales.

"The actual restoration of the locomotives was heroic too, and much praise should be heaped in particular on the now-famous 'blue team' here at Shildon whose work to convert *Dominion of Canada* to 1937 fully valanced condition complete with single chimney, chrome fittings, Canadian Pacific Bell and

Dominion of Canada back at Locomotion, where it was cosmetically restored before the first Great Gathering. ROBIN JONES

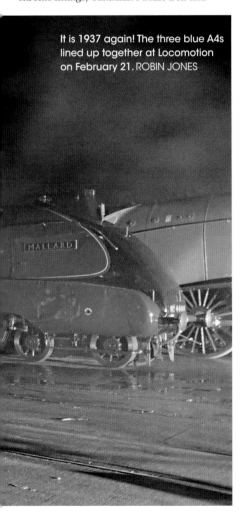

It is 1937 again! The three blue A4s lined up together at Locomotion on February 21. ROBIN JONES

For whom the bell tolls... the ceremonial bell presented to *Dominion of Canada* by that country's government is now back in place. DAVE HEWITT

Silver star: *Dominion of Canada* illuminated after the gala dinner on February 21. ROBIN JONES

Hauling a rake of brakevans on the Locomotion running line, *Bittern* passes a Northern Rail Class 142 set calling at adjacent Shildon station on the Bishop Auckland branch. Patronage of the branch services was so great at times during the Great Goodbye that it was described as akin to a Toyko commuter station in the rush hour.
ROBIN JONES

Bittern in light steam on February 21.
ROBIN JONES

chime whistle must rate as one of the more eye-catching aspects of the overall project.

"Our many sponsors and supporters pulled together magnificently, but special mention must go to Atlantic Container Line. They really were central to all this, and their calm and reassuring attitude when we missed the first planned sailing out of Halifax was just what was needed at a very stressful moment.

"I would also at this juncture wish to bring to your attention the considerable support which has been provided by Durham County Council for the events here at Shildon. At a time of considerable belt-tightening, the council understood the financial and reputational challenges of continuing to invest in Locomotion when faced with some difficult

socially focused budget reductions. But I sincerely hope that the dramatic success of Mallard 75 here at Shildon, which will have had a major impact on the county's cultural and tourism economies, has helped reinforce in your own minds the wisdom of continuing to be a major partner with the Science Museum Group in supporting and running Locomotion.

Mallard 75 went way beyond the physical confines of York and Shildon, and we should also recognise the inspired combined efforts of Network Rail, East Coast, Northern Rail, West Coast Railways, DB Schenker and many other main line operators, and of course *Bittern*'s owners, for not only facilitating a remarkable series of high-speed A4 runs but also for enabling the movement on network tracks of a

BROTHERS IN BOILERS

There has been great sadness that all good, nay utterly magnificent, things have to come to an end and the two repatriated A4s must return to their North American homes.

However, there is more to it than that. For *Dwight D. Eisenhower* and *Dominion of Canada* will return with parts once fitted to their surviving sisters in Britain.

It is often a mistake to see a locomotive as an historical artefact in itself. It is more accurate to consider that its identity was there from the day it was built. The tradition is that only the frames give the locomotive its identity.

If we cheer on Manchester United today, it may be the same club that has always been based at Old Trafford, but it is certainly not the same team as that

which turned out in, say, the 1935-36 season.

It is exactly the same with a locomotive, especially those which are members of large classes. As they are withdrawn for repairs, servicing and overhauls, a boiler from one locomotive may be given to another to allow it to 'jump the queue' and make an early return to traffic.

The Great Western Railway for one was renowned for its policy of standardised parts which could be exchanged between several classes of locomotives.

It was the same with Gresley's A4s; parts were rotated between them to such an extent that there is a quite remarkable history of the six survivors having exchanged parts.

To replace boilers deemed beyond economic repair, a large number of spare ones were built during the working lives of the A4s. During later years, these boilers were also fitted to some A3 locomotives, including most recently A3 4-6-2 No. 4472 *Flying Scotsman* during the heritage era from 1978-2006.

After being acquired by the National Railway Museum, the A4 boiler was removed, a spare A3 boiler was overhauled and the A4 boiler sold to the owner of *Bittern* for future use.

The last two batches of 25 new A4 boilers were commissioned in 1959-60. All six surviving A4s carry examples of these boilers.

Mallard today carries boiler No. 27965, which was fitted in 1961 and previously

Right: During the Great Goodbye, train operator Northern Rail laid on extra services on the Darlington to Bishop Auckland branch which serves Shildon, and produced this special free souvenir timetable leaflet.
ROBIN JONES

From opening to closing time each day, rain or shine, lengthy queues were formed by visitors who were given the chance to board the footplates of each of the five A4s, in this case *Mallard*, on static display.

fitted new to *Union of South Africa* in 1960.

Dominion of Canada now has boiler No. 27970, fitted in 1962 and previously fitted new to *Sir Nigel Gresley*.

Dwight D. Eisenhower has boiler No. 29335, fitted in 1962 and previously carried by *Bittern* in 1960.

The Great Goodbye was the last opportunity not only for six A4s to be assembled, but also for a reunion of three Diagram 107 boilers (Nos. 27965, 27970 and 29335) and the six locomotives that, between them, carried them throughout their working lives.

Furthermore, *Sir Nigel Gresley* carries several parts from No. 60026 *Miles Beevor*, including valve gear components and wheels donated when No. 60007 was

overhauled for preservation in 1967.

Since it was preserved, *Union of South Africa* has been paired with the corridor tender originally built for Gresley's experimental W1 4-6-4 No. 10000 nicknamed 'Hush Hush' because of the secrecy surrounding the project.

Tenders were of course also interchangeable. *Dominion of Canada* was fitted with four different tenders during its working life, but was paired with the same tender at both the start and end of its service, and still has the same.

By contrast, *Bittern* has always been paired with the same tender it was given as new in December 1937, but a new corridor tender body replaced the non-corridor original at its last overhaul in 2007.

The streamlined chimney cowling from *Dominion of Canada*, displayed at Locomotion during the Great Goodbye, was discharged during its reversion to 1937 condition and a replacement built.
ROBIN JONES

Bittern (left) and *Dwight D. Eisenhower* illuminated by purple lighting effects on February 21. ROBIN JONES

significant number of steam and diesel locomotives in a Mallard 75 context.

"The biggest heroes by far were Andrew Goodman and his lads from Moveright International. It is no exaggeration to say that without him and his team none of this would have happened.

"I invited Andrew in for a chat as the idea was brewing in my mind to discuss the challenges of moving locomotives across the Atlantic, and this quickly led to him

volunteering his skills and expertise. When I first saw *Dwight D. Eisenhower* hermetically sealed into its museum building in Green Bay, I was convinced the project would founder. He convinced me otherwise.

"Andrew and his team put in huge amounts of planning time while still running his day-to-day business. They were subsequently out of the country for over two months, dealing tenaciously with every problem and issue that such a complex move

could throw at them, keeping their cool, summoning every ounce of initiative, and doing their utmost to ensure that an excited and expectant British population was not disappointed.

"The Monster Moves programme was quite breathtaking in its portrayal of a man utterly determined to achieve the impossible on behalf of his country. Andrew, I and many others owe you a deep debt of gratitude. You are the star of this particular show.

No, the rival London Midland & Scottish Railway has not taken over the LNER and repainted everything crimson lake. More experimental lighting effects are in evidence on the evening of February 21. ROBIN JONES

Above: Following the all but immediate sell-out success of a limited edition of 510 models of each of the six surviving A4s under the Great Gathering badge for £169 each, a year later Mallard 75 headline sponsor Hornby produced a second set badged as the Great Goodbye, meeting with a similar response from collectors. HORNBY

Right: Those who bought all six could get a glass-fronted showcase for just £20 postage.

THE GREAT GOODBYE

NEVER AGAIN?

"Pessimistic as it may seem, I personally seriously doubt that all six A4s will be assembled in one place again. *Dwight D. Eisenhower* and *Dominion of Canada* will soon return to their native shores and to a spectacular welcome home.

"They have acted as important ambassadors for their respective owning museums and will be taking pride of place in refreshed gallery spaces where their story can be told to great effect. There will simply be no incentive for them to pay a return visit to the UK for a very long time, if ever.

"That, I'm afraid, is it.

"So let us be eternally grateful that Mallard 75 happened in our lifetimes and that so many people and organisations came together to make it happen.

"We should now use its powerful legacy to maintain the interest and enthusiasm of the many converts it achieved to the modern and heritage railway cause.

"I look forward to seeing you all at the Mallard 100 event in 2038 when I will be 79 years old!"

It has long been widely acknowledged that the National Railway Museum at York is the global leader in its field. Now the Great Goodbye has shown it too is capable of being a world platform, and the ball is now in its court to follow up on this outstanding success.

Shildon lost much of its livelihood when its railway works closed. Now it is the town's

railway heritage which could and should become its saviour.

Why, I ask, is not the whole of the route of the Stockton & Darlington Railway a designated UNESCO World Heritage Site? What other invention has done so much to shape the entire modern world as the invention and development of the steam railway locomotive in a commercially effective form? Jungles and arctic wastes apart, what corners of the world's land mass have not been affected by the impact of the opening and success of the first public steam railway? What better for Durham's economy than for the county with its phenomenal transport and industrial heritage to take its rightful place on a global stage alongside the likes of

Garter blue turns to green. *Bittern* bathed in artificial lighting on February 21. ROBIN JONES

Guests at the £70-a-head Mallard 75 gala dinner on February 21, had their own after-hours photographic session thrown in for good measure. ROBIN JONES

The final word: after Mallard 75 originator Steve Davies delivered his speech at the gala dinner, he was presented with a framed Martin Creese picture of the six A4s' line-up from four nights previously, along with a special glass plaque from Mortons Media, Britain's biggest railway magazine publisher, by *Heritage Railway* editor Robin Jones, on behalf of both the magazine and sister title *The Railway Magazine* as a thank you gesture. JAMES SHUTTLEWORTH

He was there both at the start and the end: former National Railway Museum director Steve Davies delivers his speech at the Mallard 75 gala dinner at Locomotion on February 21. ROBIN JONES

On Sunday, February 23, charter operator Steam Dreams ran a 'Cathedrals Express' tour from King's Cross to Shildon for the final afternoon of the Great Goodbye. Flying the British flag as the train climbs Stoke Bank, where *Mallard* hit 126mph in the opposite direction in 1938, is Class 47 No. 47580 *County of Essex*. MARTIN BAILEY

The 'Birdman' of Steamsong, whose operatic rendition celebrated the names of A4s named after feathered friends. ROBIN JONES

THE MALLARD OPERA!

The Great Goodbye included then part-premiere of Steamsong, a new multimedia operatic work based on the A4s. Combining the sound of an A4 chime whistle with digital sound against a backdrop of projected archive footage from the British Transport Film archive, it sets out to weave a poetic evocation of steam culture.

Composed by John Kefala Kerr, senior lecturer in music at the university of Sunderland, it has themes of industrial modernisation and utopianism – the dream of steam.

The production includes a live music ensemble led by conductor Simon Fidler and a chorus comprising members of Voices of Hope, one of the UK's leading chamber choirs, and actress Zoe Lambert.

The National Railway Museum and Durham County Council with support from the Arts Council: Grants for Arts Fund jointly commissioned John, whose previous compositions won international acclaim, to create the opera inspired by *Mallard*'s story.

In September 2013, he was appointed artist-in-residence at Locomotion exploring the meaning of *Mallard* and the A4s and developing creative and conceptual ideas for the final piece of work.

John said: "'And she jumped to it like

The premiere of a section of Steamsong, a new operatic multimedia composition by John Kefala Kerr. ROBIN JONES

a live thing' was how *Mallard*'s driver, Joe Duddington, exuberantly expressed his sense that steam engines are like living things. I've tried to do something similar with Steamsong by compressing one of railway culture's big moments into a small musical space and then releasing it again with delicacy, energy and punch."

An 18-minute extract from Steamsong was performed at the Mallard 75 gala dinner at Locomtion on February 21, with a further preview at the museum two days later, bringing together the worlds of arts and heritage as a final tribute to the A4s.

The full performance was scheduled at Durham Gala Theatre on July 12-13, 2014, as part of the Brass: Durham International Festival.

Shakespeare's birthplace and the Taj Mahal? From my perspective, it is a county of unpolished hidden jewels.

Just before closing time on February 23, a Steam Dreams 'Cathedrals Express' charter top-and-tailed by two heritage Class 47 diesels and carrying more than 300 passengers departed on its return leg to King's Cross. Sadly, it could not have been hauled by a more appropriate A4 – as they were otherwise engaged!

The next day, fans gathered at Locomotion to watch the start of the third and final break-up of the Great Gathering.

Union of South Africa coupled up to *Mallard* before towing it via the East Coast Main Line to its permanent home at York, its anniversary celebrations finally over.

Sharon Thorburn, Locomotion's front of office manager, said: "Everyone seems to have been really amazed by the display and now that they're going it seems such a shame."

With *Sir Nigel Gresley* leaving the following day and *Bittern* the day after that, the repatriated pair were left on their own.

Visitors to Locomotion were still able to see them until Easter, after which they were scheduled for their return transatlantic voyage from Liverpool around early May, the reverse of their outward journey as described in detail in Mallard 75 the book. Again, the man masterminding the return trip was Andrew Goodman of Moveright International.

After being unloaded at Halifax in Nova Scotia, they were to be transported on the back

The glow from an A4 firebox concluded the preview extract of Steamsong on February 21. ROBIN JONES

The party is over: *Union of South Africa* propels its support coach and *Mallard* out of the Locomotion yard and on to the Bishop Auckland branch on Monday, February 24. ANTHONY COULLS

of flat cars to No. 4489's home, the Exporail museum in Montreal.

There, the pair were to be posed for one last picture before being split apart again, possibly for the last time ever, with *Dwight D. Eisenhower* returning to its home in Green Bay and bringing the last vestiges of the Great Gathering to a final close.

Will all six ever meet again?

Never say never – because you run the risk of a man like Steve Davies deciding otherwise!

■ **Thanks to charter operator Steam Dreams for help in compiling this chapter. Details of its extensive main line tour programme can be seen at www.steamdreams.co.uk or telephone 01483 209888 for more details.**

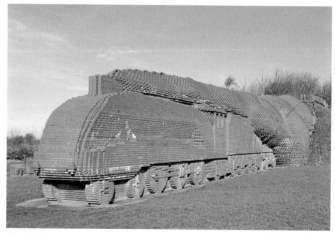

One A4 that will not be moving from County Durham, let alone going across the Atlantic, is this brick sculpture on the eastern outskirts of Darlington, a few miles from Locomotion. Named Train, it is the work of artist David Mach and was unveiled by Lord Palumbo of Walbrook on June 23, 1997. ROBIN JONES

Bittern, the last of the four British A4s at the Great Goodbye crosses Yarm viaduct after leaving Shildon on Wednesday, February 26, 2014. STUART BROWN

Union of South Africa tows Mallard through Northallerton on Monday, February 24, 2014, en route from Shildon to the National Railway Museum at York. JONATHAN MORLEY

A4 Sir Nigel Gresley can be regularly seen in action just over half an hour's journey by car from Locomotion. This superb 5in scale model is based at the Teesside Small Gauge Railway, which has a 1200ft circuit in Preston Park, Stockton-on-Tees. TSGR

Mallard back inside the National Railway Museum at York, ready to be shunted back into its permanent display position. NRM

4468

The Magnificent Seven

The Great Goodbye was not the first time that Locomotion had hosted a line-up of surviving members of a cutting-edge East Coast Main Line locomotive class.

On Friday, September 7, 2011, the venue held a unique gathering of all seven surviving Deltic diesels – the successors to the A4s and the other LNER Pacifics. The award-winning event was organised by the Deltic Preservation Society to mark the 50th anniversary of the production Class 55s.

The line-up saw the National Railway Museum's prototype Deltic DP1 gathered together with all six preserved production Deltics, No. 55002 *The King's Own Yorkshire Light Infantry*, No. 55019 *Royal Highland Fusilier*, D9016 *Gordon Highlander*, D9009 *Alycidon*, No. 55022 *Royal Scots Grey*, and

D9015 *Tulyar*.

Britain was late in replacing steam with diesel and electric traction. Gresley beat off the challenge from the likes of the German Flying Hamburger railcar set with his A4s, showing that steam could still win the day in terms of speed, but back in the Thirties, it was clear to many that the writing was on the wall.

It was only postwar austerity that prevented Britain from not following the US, Ireland and other countries in modernising its railway system and dispensing with steam much earlier. Had it done so, the A4s might have been gone before the Sixties. As it was, most saw less than three decades in traffic.

On December 1, 1954, the Modernisation and Re-Equipment of the British Railways, or the 1955 Modernisation Plan for short, was

published, calling for the elimination of steam locomotives as soon as possible. It prompted a free-for-all among locomotive designers and builders in a bid to come up with new types of diesel and electric traction.

In 1942, English Electric took over engine builder D Napier & Son on the instruction of the Ministry of Aircraft Production. The firm looked into the possibility of using Napier's Deltic engine, which had previously been used in ships, to power a new type of railway locomotive.

In 1954-55, a prototype locomotive incorporating two of these Deltic engines was built at English Electric's Dick Kerr works in Preston. Owned by its builder, it was officially numbered DP1 (Diesel Prototype No. 1) and, finished in powder blue livery with cream stripes, carried the word Deltic in large capital letters on its sides.

Its distinctive front whiskers drew on the style of contemporary American diesels, as the manufacturer was also thinking of the export market. A large continental-style lamp was fitted to the nose at either end.

DP1 underwent trials on the London Midland Region in October 1955, working between London and Liverpool, and also on the Settle and Carlisle line, but officials lost interest when it became clear that the West Coast Main Line was to be electrified. However, the Eastern Region welcomed it with open arms, as until then nobody had produced a blueprint for a diesel which could better Gresley's Pacifics, especially the A4s.

Like the A4 Pacifics, their successors the Deltics were all named. Locomotives Finsbury Park locomotives like D9015 *Tuylar,* pictured at Locomotion, took the names of winning racehorses, as per the LNER naming tradition with the A3s – after all, they were destined to be used over Stoke Bank, the steam era's greatest racetrack. Meanwhile, the Deltics based at Haymarket and Gateshead were named after British army regiments.
ROBIN JONES

After DP1 successfully underwent trials mainly between King's Cross and Doncaster, British Railways was so impressed that it ordered 22 production versions from English Electric, all built between 1961-62.

DP1 suffered a serious powerplant failure in March 1961 and was taken out of service permanently. Plans to test it on Canadian railways failed to materialise, and so it was cosmetically restored and donated to the Science Museum,

The introduction of the production Deltics did not go smoothly, and drivers complained about draughty doors which in some cases would not stay closed, slippery cab and engine room floors which quickly became contaminated with oil, and boiler and oil pressure switch problems. There were instances of Deltics being taken off their trains at Peterborough or Grantham and replaced by A4s, A3s, or V2s. However, the problems were soon sorted.

They were delivered in a smart two-tone green, a livery which still kept one foot in the steam age. The dark British Railways green on top, with a narrower strip of a lighter, lime green along the bottom, with white for the cab window surrounds. British Railways quickly applied the bright yellow warning panel typical to diesel and electric locomotives at each end.

In 1964, British Railways unveiled its new corporate blue livery. With a few years, all regional steam era liveries were replaced by a one-size-fits-all Rail Blue or blue and white livery, adopted by the Deltics from 1966 onwards, again with the yellow warning panels. With the introduction of BR's TOPS computer system, they were renumbered 55001 to 55022 as Class 55.

The Deltics were a marked improvement on the Class 40 diesels which had earlier been introduced to the ECML. The 40s had a maximum drawbar horsepower of 1450, which could be exceeded by a Pacific steam locomotive if worked hard.

By 1963 Deltics were recorded as exceeding 100mph. The late railway writer O S Nock recorded 100mph for 16 miles south of Thirsk with a maximum of 104mph, and said that such speeds in 1963 were "terrific".

By the mid-Sixties the Deltic-hauled 'Flying Scotsman' was achieving a five hour, 55 minute, timing from King's Cross to Edinburgh with one stop at Newcastle. It was the fastest-ever timing, beating the prewar A4 hauled 'Coronation' service's six hours. With upgrades to the ECML, the timing fell to five hours 30 minutes by the mid-Seventies.

On February 2, 1978, No. 55008 *The Green Howards* hauled 10 coaches comprising the 7.25am from Newcastle to King's Cross and set new records. On the leg from York to London it achieved a timing of 137 minutes 15 seconds, including signal stops and speed reductions. The estimated running time of 115 min 45 seconds gave an average of 97mph start to stop. No. 55008 achieved 113mph on the flat between Darlington and York, 114mph at Offord… and 125mph while descending where else but Stoke Bank!

By the late Seventies, the Deltics had a new rival on the route in the form of the Class 43 High Speed Train, branded as InterCity 125. The Seventies marked another major shift in British Rail stock policy, with the large-scale introduction of diesel railcars and multiple units in the Fifties having begun the elimination of run-round loops and associated stock movements.

The Deltics began to take on secondary roles, but the end was nigh. British Rail had a general policy of not maintaining small nonstandard fleets of locomotives, and so a class of just 22 had a limited future. The end of the decade saw the first withdrawals from service, and subsequent scrapping at Doncaster.

The final Deltic run under British Rail was the 4.30pm Aberdeen-York service on December 31, 1981, hauled from Edinburgh by No. 55019. The last train was an enthusiast special, the 'Deltic Scotsman Farewell' on January 2, 1982, from King's Cross to Edinburgh and back, hauled by No. 55015 *Tulyar* northbound and No. 55022 *Royal Scots Grey* on the return. Six found their way into preservation: others ended up at Doncaster where A4s had been broken on the scrap line less than 20 years before.

The Deltic record would be bettered by the Class 43s. The prototype InterCity 125 (comprising power cars Nos. 43000 and 43001) set the world record for diesel traction at 143.2mph on the ECML on June 12, 1973.

More great shades of *Mallard* were to follow. The world speed record for a diesel train carrying passengers was set on September 27, 1985, during a special press launch of a new Tees-Tyne Pullman service from Newcastle to King's Cross, formed of a shortened 2+5 set, which reached 144mph north of York.

The world record for the fastest diesel-powered train was set on November 1, 1987, by a HST set comprising power cars No. 43102 *City of Wakefield* and No. 43104 and three carriages.

The set reached 148mph as it descended, yes, you guessed, Stoke Bank on a test run for a new type of bogie later to be used by Mark 4 coaches.

HSTs are still very much in service on the ECML, more than four decades after the prototype appeared. They have lasted in regular traffic around a decade more than the A4s did and twice as long as the Deltics, and are considered one of the most successful types of British railway traction of all time.

Blue is again the colour: grabbing attention on the East Coast Main Line two decades after *Mallard's* world record feat was prototype Deltic DP1, pictured outside Locomotion on September 7, 2011.
ROBIN JONES

CHAPTER SIXTEEN

A new Gresley masterpiece for the 21st century

There was much sadness when, at close of play on Sunday, February 23, the final curtain came down on the Great Goodbye. It marked the end to one of the most phenomenal episodes in the history of railway preservation, one which had gripped the public imagination in ways that few of the originators of the project had dared to hope.

There were many sceptics who refused to believe that *Dwight D. Eisenhower* and *Dominion of Canada* would ever return to these shores, and doubts lingered until October 3, 2012, when the pair were offloaded at Liverpool's Seaforth Dock.

That evening, views on *Heritage Railway*'s www.heritagerailway.com website and www.facebook.com/heritagerailway page shot through the roof. Yes, the promised miracle had happened.

Since then, both of those sites have been regularly filled with the often-heard comment from the enthusiast linesides – "Why can't they stay over here?"

Indeed, at least one major blank chequebook offer has been made to buy one or both of the expatriate A4s with a view to restoration to running order, but has been rebuffed, like the many offers to buy them and bring them back over the past half century.

The arguments are the same – nameplates apart, they have got nothing to do with the history of the US or Canada, by and large railway enthusiasts are interested only in the locomotives with a traditional outline relating to their own country, the sale could help finance the restoration of North American locomotives and so on. Here in Britain, they would be appreciated by millions of people…

It is easy to have great sympathy with such arguments, but one basic fact cannot be avoided. If not for the US National Railroad Museum at Green Bay, Wisconsin, and the Exporail museum at Montreal, these A4s would have gone the way of the 28 other A4s withdrawn by British Railways and been turned into razor blades.

We British today might love the art deco A4s, but back in the mid-Sixties we hardly lifted a finger to save them from being scrapped –

familiarity brought contempt, the end of steam was unavoidable and all that. Disgracefully, we could not save even the first of the class, No. 2509 *Silver Link*.

Nobody today, of course, would ever consider scrapping an A4, but back then, times were different. The preservation movement was still at an embryonic stage, and those precious few who sought to preserve what they could of steam were still feeling their way in pitch blackness.

Therefore, we owe a massive debt of gratitude to the North American museums, for the survival of these two A4s and also for making the dream of the three Great Gatherings (and the Barrow Hill Roundhouse visit) possible.

Their reward is two examples of the world's fastest class of steam locomotives restored to pristine condition. Back across the Atlantic, they will hold the torch for Thirties cutting edge British transport technology, while cementing a fresh relationship between preservation sectors an ocean apart.

Let us not bemoan the departure of No. 4489 and No. 60008, but instead celebrate Sir Nigel

COCK O' THE NORTH

P2 No. 2001 *Cock O' The North* in LNER service. P2SLC Inset: One of the nameplates from *Cock O' The North* was displayed during Doncaster Museum & Art Gallery's, Mallard - a Doncaster Thoroughbred, exhibition. ROBIN JONES

Gresley's masterpieces – by building a new one.

We have been delighted by the sight of all six surviving examples of the world's fastest steam locomotive type together.

Now let's create the seventh example of Britain's most powerful express passenger steam locomotive – Gresley's P2 2-8-2.

As the two North American A4s were being prepared for their return trip, plans were in hand to cut the frames – the single component which gives a locomotive its identity – for the new P2, No. 2007 *Prince of Wales*.

Artist's impression of the seventh Gresley P2, No. 2007 *Prince of Wales*.

THE GRESLEY MIKADOS

Sir Nigel Gresley's P2s were conceived to haul heavy trains over the Edinburgh to Aberdeen line.

The original scheme combined the 2-8-2 wheel arrangement with an A3 boiler but this was subsequently worked up into a design with a longer firebox and double chimney.

The mechanical innovations of the P2s were matched by their bold outward appearance.

The doyen of the class, No. 2001 *Cock o' the North*, was radically equipped with Lentz rotary valve gear (the inventor was Hugo Lenz, but it was patented as Lentz to make it easier for English-speaking people), an ACFI feed water heater in place of the exhaust steam injector (the locomotive still retained one injector on the driver's side), a 50sq ft firegrate and streamlined steam passages to three cylinders that exhausted via a double Kylchap chimney.

Gresley was greatly influenced by the work of French engineer André Chapelon who had pioneered the use of these features and was determined to incorporate them in the P2s. Externally, the design hid the tapered boiler in a parallel, elliptical cladding running from a V-fronted cab to a muscular, streamlined smokebox (which incorporated integrated smoke deflectors), the whole affair sitting on a high running board which exposed the 6ft 2in drivers entirely.

The 220psi boiler fed three 21in x 26in cylinders and the locomotive developed a nominal tractive effort of 43,460lb. As a final touch, *Cock o' the North* was the first LNER locomotive to carry a chime whistle.

The second member of the class, No. 2002 *Earl Marischal*, was fitted with Walschaerts valve gear and was later equipped with additional smoke deflectors to compensate for the softer exhaust resulting from its use.

The final four members of this small class, No. 2003 *Lord President*, No. 2004 *Mons Meg*, No. 2005 *Thane of Fife* and No. 2006 *Wolf of Badenoch*, all appeared with an A4 (streamlined) front end coupled with the elliptical boiler cladding of the first two.

Only No. 2001 was equipped with the feed water heater and this was removed when Nos. 2001 and 2002 were later rebuilt with the A4 front end.

No. 2001 *Cock o' the North* entered traffic in May 1934 and was tested on various routes in England and Scotland, in consequence small adjustments were made to the exhaust cams in the poppet valve gear and an oil circulation system was incorporated for the camboxes.

In December of that year the locomotive was sent to a new test plant at Vitry-sur-Seine for evaluation.

While in France the locomotive also hauled test trains with a dynamometer car and produced some impressive runs, recording in excess of 2000dbhp. Also in France, the optimum dimensions for the blast arrangement were finalised and Kylchap assembly set.

Back in Britain No. 2001 was put to work in Scotland, followed shortly by the other members of the class. The locomotives did prodigious work hauling 550-tonne trains on the Aberdeen route.

As noted before, *Cock o' the North* and *Earl Marischal* were both equipped with the A4 front end and when No. 2001 was at Doncaster in 1937 for this work the opportunity was taken to fit the locomotive with Walschaerts valve gear as well as removing the feed water heater.

As a small class requiring higher than average attention it inevitably came under close scrutiny from Edward Thompson, the LNER's new chief mechanical engineer following Sir Nigel Gresley's premature death, and he decided to rebuild all six P2s as A2/2 Pacifics during 1944.

Thus the magnificent Mikados effectively became extinct, the final blow falling when the rebuilt engines were scrapped in 1961.

WHAT NEXT AFTER *TORNADO*?

On January 31, 2009, Peppercorn A1 Pacific No. 60163 *Tornado* made its debut on the main line, generating international headlines, for it was the first new steam locomotive built for use on the British national network since British Railways Standard 9F 2-1-0-0 No. 92220 *Evening Star* was outshopped from Swindon in 1960.

Tornado was officially named by the Prince of Wales and the Duchess of Cornwall at York station on February 19 that year, and afterwards hauled the Royal Train for the first time.

The new A1 – the 50th of the type to be built, filling a gap left by the scrapping of the rest in the Sixties – was a project that took 19 years from a few mates getting around a table to discuss a steam 'wish list' to its triumphant appearance on the East Coast Main Line, after £3 million had been raised to finance it.

As the project progressed over that time, the snowball effect kicked in. As first, like the repatriation of the A4s, labelled as pipe dream, more and more supporters came on board as visible progress was made, many becoming covenantors of builder, The A1 Steam Locomotive Trust, and donating a regular monthly amount towards its construction.

The proof of the quality of the project is there for all to see. Now that the dream has become

P2 Steam Locomotive Company chairman, Mark Allatt, and Prince Charles at the official launch of A1 Pacific No. 60163 *Tornado* into traffic at York on February 19, 2009. ROBIN JONES

P2 company chairman Mark Allatt said: "Prince Charles has been a fantastic supporter of *Tornado* and along with the Duchess of Cornwall formally named the new locomotive in 2009. Since then, *Tornado* has hauled the Royal Train on no fewer than three occasions on behalf of Prince Charles, so we are only too delighted to be able to confirm the name for No.2007 in his honour. It is well known HRH has a passion for our heritage as well as a particular interest in steam and the skills and craftsmanship required to build a steam locomotive from scratch."

How the new Gresley P2 No. 2007 will appear. P2SLC Inset: The nameplate for the new P2. P2SLC

reality, and many trails have been blazed to overcome all the hurdles to make it happen, not least of all the single-most important aspect, the fundraising, it became clear that a second project could be completed in a far shorter time.

Many members of The A1 Steam Locomotive Trust had long held the ambition of building a P2, a Gresley design which, unlike his A4s, was never fully developed, before they were rebuilt by Thompson into ungainly 4-6-2s in 1944. Indeed, the intention to follow an A1 with a P2 was first made public on June 24, 1994.

Following a feasibility study into the construction of a new P2 – which examined the commercial, engineering and certification challenges that would be faced – The P2 Steam Locomotive Company (a subsidiary of The A1 Steam Locomotive Trust) was formed to bring the project to life.

THE NEW P2

The mission is to develop, build and operate an improved Gresley P2 Mikado steam locomotive for main line and preserved railway use.

The P2SLC will build the seventh member of class, demonstrating how the potential of the most powerful class of express passenger steam locomotives to operate in the UK can at long last be fully realised.

The builders will use modern computer design and modelling techniques to enable it to deliver its true potential hauling passenger trains at high speed across the national network.

The new locomotive's design will be aesthetically similar to P2 No. 2001 *Cock O' The North*, as it is a construction and development project not an opportunity for major redesign.

The P2 project will make maximum use of systems, fittings and processes in use on No. 60163 *Tornado*: any changes to the original design will be either for operational, manufacturing or certification reasons.

The design will take into account the needs of the operator, and all decisions will be judged on their value for money. It will meet current and foreseeable regulatory standards to allow the locomotive to operate as intended.

The new Gresley class P2 will, like *Tornado* be numbered as the next in the series – No. 2007 – and will be named *Prince of Wales*.

As with *Tornado*, three vital decisions have been taken.

Funding is a priority; the team leading the project are professionals in relevant fields so that their work for the project will be to the highest standards; and, because of reasons of certification and the nature of the work being undertaken, the majority of the manufacture of the locomotive will be undertaken by the engineering industry.

The team behind *Prince of Wales* include the key people behind the building and operation of Tornado as well as a number of new people. The project team is based around four principles:

It will be run using the best business practices by people experienced in the appropriate areas.

The primary funding method will be simple, and capable of being understood and afforded by anyone. The enormity of the task means there will have to be a single aim to focus on, the project's mission statement: "The development

P2 No. 2001 *Cock O' The North* at the test plant at Vitry-sur-Seine in December 1934. P2SLC

and building of an improved Gresley class P2" against which all proposed actions will be judged.

The rules of the organisation prohibit cliques and any form of elitism. Everyone will achieve recognition based on effort rather than size of chequebook. This enables all efforts to go into the building of the new P2.

A nationwide management team has been put together consisting of people who freely give considerable amounts of time and expertise. As with *Tornado*, the P2SLC is fortunate to be supported by a wide range of specialists, experts and enthusiasts from all walks of life.

RAISING THE MONEY

The P2SLC estimates that No. 2007 will cost around £5 million to build over a seven to 10-year period. As worked successfully with *Tornado*, funds to build No. 2007 *Prince of Wales* will be raised through regular monthly donations (covenants), donations dedicated to specific components, commercial sponsorship, loans and a bond issue. The company is also working to secure the backing of the best of British businesses for the project.

In order to compress the build time from the 18 years it took with *Tornado*, before it underwent its first trial runs on the Great Central Railway in the summer of 2008, to just seven years for *Prince of Wales*, the project needs a 'running-start' and an initial target of £100,000 was set.

The P2SLC therefore established the Founders Club – a group of early supporters each donating £1000 (in up to four payments of £250 by standing order) and the funds are being

used to get to the project to the point of cutting No. 2007 *Prince of Wales*'s frames and ordering other major components.

The Founders Club was launched at the A1SLT's convention on September 21, 2013 and after only four weeks had raised the required initial £100,000 – a figure that took around four years to raise for *Tornado*. By February 2014, more than £300,000 (when Gift Aid is taken into account due to the Trust's charitable status) had been raised from 250 people from as far afield as North America, Australia and Europe.

The main fundraising campaign was launched in March 2014 when members of the Founders Club were given the chance to become the first P2 covenantors.

BUILDING NO. 2007 *PRINCE OF WALES*

In much the same way that *Tornado* was constructed as the 50th Peppercorn class A1 rather than a replica of the original members of the class, No. 2007 *Prince of Wales* will be the seventh member of the P2 class, likewise allowing for improvements and variations in design. The decision to closely follow the pattern set by *Cock o' the North* means that the locomotive will have the original and distinctive semi-streamlining and rotary cam valve gear and will look, to all intents and purposes, like No. 2001.

However, it is acknowledged that the original P2s had certain weaknesses and No. 2007 will have these eliminated at the design stage. Some fundamental criteria have already been decided:

Frames: The foundation of any locomotive will incorporate a modified leading pony truck to

A computer-generated image of P2 No. 2007 *Prince of Wales*. P2SLC

Above: Drawing for the P2's pony truck assembly. P2SLC

Right: Close up of part of the planned frame assembly for the seventh Gresley P2. P2SLC

The initial drawing for the frame assembly of No. 2007 *Prince of Wales*.

Grey – existing P2 design unaltered

Green – existing A1 Tornado design incorporated – rear frames, roller bearing axles and axleboxes

Yellow – original P2 design requiring minor changes (spring hanger brackets)

Red – P2 frame stays requiring significant re-design to accommodate air brakes

(original P2s were fitted with vacuum brakes only)

Turquoise – start of new cylinder block design as a fabricated welded steel monobloc with reduced cylinder diameter to fit modern loading gauge for use with 250psi boiler and changes to

suit British Caprotti valve gear derived from that used on No. 71000 *Duke of Gloucester*.

Purple – adapted postwar spring side control V2 pony truck to address the known track force problems with the original P2 Gresley swing link design. P2SLC

avoid the issues that afflicted the original P2s in this area. The LNER solved the problem when the V2s showed a similar tendency and computer modelling is being used to redesign a more stable arrangement. There will also be a modification to side clearances to allow improved performance on curves.

Wheel sets and running gear: Unlike the originals, No. 2007 will have roller bearings throughout – experience with those fitted to No. 60163 has vindicated the choice for that locomotive already. Many of the patterns will be common to both *Tornado* and *Prince of Wales* and thus save a lot of expense – indeed a spare cannon box already exists.

A critical failure area on the original P2s was the crank axle. It is considered that modern principles will be adopted in the redesign of this critical area.

Larger diameter components and the use of roller bearings are considered beneficial, and more modern techniques avoid stress points and relieve fatigue points. For a simpler manufacturing technique, all driving wheels will be cast from the same pattern with fabricated balance weights being employed.

Cylinders and valve gear: The idea to model No. 2007 on *Cock o' the North* means that rotary valve gear is preferable. Changes will be made to the cylinder diameter, reducing it to 19.75in

to compensate for the increased boiler pressure available from the 250psi diagram 118A fitted to *Tornado*.

However, the Lentz gear used on the original during its tests at Vitry offered only limited cut-off settings and may have contributed, in part, to No. 2001's high coal consumption. Gresley D49 4-4-0 *The Morpeth* had infinitely variable Reidinger gear (a development of Lentz with some features of Caprotti valves) fitted in the 1930s. When rebuilt by Thompson, this was fitted to *The Garth*, which ran successfully in service, until 1958.

In order to benefit from the variable cut-off, the P2SLC is also considering British Caprotti valve gear using a derived drive for the centre cylinder.

This valve gear was perfected in its application to BR Standard 8P Pacific No. 71000 *Duke of Gloucester* and offers infinitely variable cut-off. However, a critical challenge not yet resolved is the Caprotti valve operation for the centre cylinder. The arrangement on *Duke of Gloucester* is not compatible with the cylinder and drive layout of a P2. This problem taxed Gresley and he chose to split the inlet and exhaust valve chests.

The final stages of the examination of both the Lentz and British Caprotti options for No. 2007's valve gear were underway in

February 2014. Drawing work has continued on the Caprotti option to work up a design that would fit on the P2.

At the same time the P2SLC is investigating the original Lentz gear and its development by the Franklin Railway Supply Company (a subsidiary of Lima Locomotive Works) of the US where evidence shows that locomotives worked successfully with infinitely variable cams to the end of steam in the US. Although there's increasing confidence that the latter will provide the solution that the P2SLC is looking for, there is, of course, always the option of Walschaerts/Gresley valve gear as eventually fitted to all six of the originals.

Subject to final design, it is likely that the cylinders will be fabricated, as long as the streamlined steam passages can be replicated.

The original P2 design included nickel steel coupling and connecting rods. Given understanding in this area has shown nickel steel as having more potential for failure, carbon/manganese steel similar to that used on *Tornado* will be employed. This may lead to a slight change in profile and section of these rods.

Boiler: Although the original class had 220psi boilers the overall size is similar to the diagram 118A 250psi boiler fitted to No. 60163, thus giving the option to interchange this component at overhauls. The P2 boilers

FIRST STEPS

TV presenter James May threw his weight behind the P2 project when he agreed to make the first component himself.

P2SLC/A1SLT chairman, Mark Allatt, has known James since the Top Gear team raced *Tornado* from King's Cross to Edinburgh on April 25, 2009. James drove a Jaguar XK120 of similar vintage to the original Peppercorn A1s while Jeremy Clarkson acted as fireman on *Tornado*.

Furthermore, in an episode of James May's Toy Stories, with the help of Hornby he relaid the line from Barnstaple to Bideford in OO scale. His recruitment to the P2 is viewed as another major publicity coup.

While the Great Goodbye was attracting record crowds a few miles to the north, James turned up at The A1 Steam Locomotive Trust's Darlington Locomotive Works on Thursday, February 20, and made the smoke box dart, the component that keeps the smoke box door securely closed. The external portion of the dart is the familiar feature that resembles the hands on a clock face.

He said: "Not many man-made machines stir the soul, but a full-blown steam locomotive is right up there, and we invented it. However, over the decades we've lost so much of the talent, skill and knowledge needed to build them.

"That's why it's such a thrill to work alongside the team building No. 2007 *Prince of Wales*, determined to not only resurrect this monster from the past, but also to improve it using modern wizardry. It's a real privilege to know that when *Prince of Wales* eventually roars past me at a station, I can proudly say along with many others that I helped build that… and it works!

The A1/P2 team and James May with the finished article. P2SLC

"The whole spectrum of manufacturing brilliance will be represented in the P2. At one end, boffins will program computerised plasma-cutters to produce – more accurately than could have been imagined originally – the massive frames of the engine's chassis.

"At the other, someone might produce a small control handle at a bench, using just a vice and a few simple files in a scene that has gone largely unchanged for two centuries."

The same month it was announced that the frames had been ordered, with an order placed with Tata Steel, a significant partner in the project.

Mark Allatt said: "We are delighted that James agreed to craft the first part of No. 2007 *Prince of Wales*. James has been a fervent supporter of ours over the years with *Tornado* and we are very pleased to have him on board with our next adventure to build the most powerful steam locomotive to operate in the UK. This isn't the first time James has got his hands dirty with us; he has been out as a volunteer member of *Tornado's* support crew, helping ensure the locomotive ran smoothly.

"Thanks to the magnitude of support generated in only four months from the Founders Club, we are in the enviable position of securing major elements of the locomotive much earlier and quicker than we forecast and also we have been able to demonstrate to key industry partners the validity of this project.

"Our journey to bring Britain's most powerful steam locomotive back from the annals of history is coming that much closer to reality."

James proudly displays the finished smokebox cover dart. P2SLC

James May cutting the first component for the new Gresley P2 on a lathe inside Darlington Locomotive Works on February 20, 2014. P2SLC

were 17in longer overall compared with diagram 118. Also, No. 2006 *Wolf of Badenoch* had a longer combustion chamber – the earlier engines had a short combustion chamber.

The P2 varied in some regards to the A1 in the area of the ashpan and grate, but these would, for servicing advantages, follow those on the A1.

The locomotive will have Davies and Metcalfe exhaust steam injector rather than a feed water heater (removed from No. 2001 in 1938). Compared with the A1, a larger K class injector would be selected. A pre-war Crosby chime whistle will be fitted as per No. 2001 *Cock O' The North* – the first to so be fitted.

Tender: It is proposed that the tender will be identical to that used by *Tornado*, featuring the modifications that allow more water and slightly less coal to be carried. It will run on roller bearings and will have spoked wheels.

A review of enabling longer fire irons to be carried, and a modification to the tender front lockers to make space for the ERTMS cab signalling equipment will be completed before construction. It should be noted that No. 2001 had an experimental all-welded tender tank and spoked wheels, so

authenticity is retained.

Cab: The cab will follow the design of No. 2001 and No. 2002 with small cut out (as from 1935 onwards), A4 seats, a wraparound rear platework and full beading. The cab will be reduced to 13ft and fitted with A1 type spring doors. A final design change will seek to reduce the effects of the safety valves inside the cab.

Ancillaries: Braking will follow the design perfected during the construction of No. 60163, primary air brakes for locomotive and train with secondary vacuum brakes for working preserved stock. A consideration of improving the design of air production will be looked at during the project.

The electrical system will copy the system fitted to *Tornado*, although the original P2s did not have a Stone's generator or electric lighting. It is proposed to locate the turbo generator in the location that the water heater pumps occupied. The heater was contained in the casing over the top of the boiler with the pipes to it behind the blister on the fireman's side.

PROGRESS TO DATE

Design & certification: Contracts are now in place with Delta Rail and Lloyds Register Rail. The former will complete the engineering studies needed to enable No. 2007 to operate on the national network, and the latter is the organisation that will approve the process and principles of construction. Both are critical steps.

Frames: work has continued on the main frames in 3D Solidworks with the Cartazzi hornblocks

and additional details of spring gear added to the drawing. Materials have now been specified and an order for the mainframes is imminent.

Cylinders & motion: Examinations are now in the final stages of both the Lentz and British Caprotti options for No. 2007's valve gear. Drawing work has continued on the Caprotti option to work up a design that would fit on the P2.

At the same time investigations are underway on the original Lentz gear and its development by the Franklin Railway Supply Company where evidence shows that locomotives worked successfully with infinitely variable cams to the end of steam in the US.

Recent 3D design work has concentrated on supporting the Delta Rail assignment – including wheels, connecting and coupling rods, crossheads and slide bars – and will establish the maximum allowable side clearances in axle boxes in order to improve low-speed negotiation of curves.

TIME TO GET ON BOARD…

As part of the design process, the P2SLC is researching the history of the P2s and No. 2001 *Cock O' The North* in particular.

The company has already discovered a number of unpublished gems but officials believe that there is a lot more out there.

If anyone has any documents relating to or photographs of P2s, the company would be delighted to hear from you – especially from anyone with first-hand experience of them before they were rebuilt in 1944.

■ For more information on the project to build Gresley P2 No. 2007 *Prince of Wales* and how to get involved please visit www.p2steam.com email enquiries@p2steam.com or follow The P2 Steam Locomotive Company on Facebook and Twitter.

The company has the expertise, the track record and a plan…

But it can't happen without you.

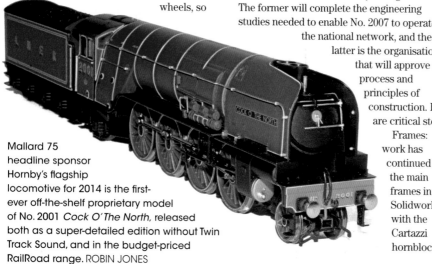

Mallard 75 headline sponsor Hornby's flagship locomotive for 2014 is the first-ever off-the-shelf proprietary model of No. 2001 *Cock O' The North,* released both as a super-detailed edition without Twin Track Sound, and in the budget-priced RailRoad range. ROBIN JONES